Alan Titchmarsh
how to garden

Climbers and
Wall Shrubs

Alan
Titchmarsh
how to garden

Climbers and
Wall Shrubs

BOOKS

Published in 2010 by BBC Books, an imprint of
Ebury Publishing, a Random House Group Company

The Random House Group Limited Reg. No. 954009

Addresses for companies within the Random House
Group can be found at
www.randomhouse.co.uk

The Random House Group Limited supports The Forest
Stewardship Council (FSC), the leading international
forest certification organisation. All our titles that are
printed on Greenpeace approved FSC certified paper
carry the FSC logo. Our paper procurement policy can
be found at www.rbooks.co.uk/environment

A CIP catalogue record for this book is available from
the British Library.

ISBN 978 1 84 6074035

Produced by OutHouse!
Shalbourne, Marlborough, Wiltshire SN8 3QJ

BBC BOOKS
COMMISSIONING EDITOR: Lorna Russell
PROJECT EDITOR: Caroline McArthur
PRODUCTION: Lucy Harrison

OUTHOUSE!
CONCEPT DEVELOPMENT & SERIES DESIGN:
  Elizabeth Mallard-Shaw, Sharon Cluett
PROJECT MANAGEMENT: Polly Boyd, Sue Gordon
ART DIRECTOR: Robin Whitecross
CONTRIBUTING EDITOR: Jonathan Edwards
PROJECT EDITOR: Anna Kruger
DESIGNER: Heather McCarry
ILLUSTRATOR: Lizzie Harper

PHOTOGRAPHS by Jonathan Buckley except where
credited otherwise on page 128

Colour origination by Altaimage, London
Printed and bound by Firmengruppe APPL,
Wemding, Germany

Contents

Introduction

Gardening is one of the best and most fulfilling activities on earth, but it can sometimes seem complicated and confusing. The answers to problems can usually be found in books, but big fat gardening books can be rather daunting. Where do you start? How can you find just the information you want without wading through lots of stuff that is not appropriate to your particular problem? Well, a good index is helpful, but sometimes a smaller book devoted to one particular subject fits the bill better – especially if it is reasonably priced and if you have a small garden where you might not be able to fit in everything suggested in a larger volume.

The *How to Garden* books aim to fill that gap – even if sometimes it may be only a small one. They are clearly set out and written, I hope, in a straightforward, easy-to-understand style. I don't see any point in making gardening complicated, when much of it is based on common sense and observation. (All the key techniques are explained and illustrated, and I've included plenty of tips and tricks of the trade.)

There are suggestions on the best plants and the best varieties to grow in particular situations and for a particular effect. I've tried to keep the information crisp and to the point so that you can find what you need quickly and easily and then put your new-found knowledge into practice. Don't worry if you're not familiar with the Latin names of plants. They are there to make sure you can find the plant as it will be labelled in the nursery or garden centre, but where appropriate I have included common names, too. Forgetting a plant's name need not stand in your way when it comes to being able to grow it.

Above all, the *How to Garden* books are designed to fill you with passion and enthusiasm for your garden and all that its creation and care entails, from designing and planting it to maintaining it and enjoying it. For more than fifty years gardening has been my passion, and that initial enthusiasm for watching plants grow, for trying something new and for just being outside pottering has never faded. If anything I am keener on gardening now than I ever was and get more satisfaction from my plants every day. It's not that I am simply a romantic, but rather that I have learned to look for the good in gardens and in plants, and there is lots to be found. Oh, there are times when I fail – when my plants don't grow as well as they should and I need to try harder. But where would I rather be on a sunny day? Nowhere!

The *How to Garden* handbooks will, I hope, allow some of that enthusiasm – childish though it may be – to rub off on you, and the information they contain will, I hope, make you a better gardener, as well as opening your eyes to the magic of plants and flowers.

Introducing climbers and wall shrubs

Climbers and wall shrubs produce show-stopping displays of flowers, fruits and foliage that stimulate all the senses. They're very useful around the garden, too, breaking up stark walls and covering eyesores as well as providing a welcome colour boost to lacklustre trees and shrubs. They're such a diverse bunch that there's a climber or wall shrub for every situation, no matter where you live or what soil you have. Best of all, they can even be squeezed into well-established gardens that are already crammed with plants.

What are climbers and wall shrubs?

Climbers and wall shrubs are among the most indispensable and versatile plants in the garden. They can be used in diverse ways and in many situations, making themselves at home in the smallest urban courtyard as well as the largest country garden. They will provide you with colour and interest at any time of the year and introduce height into your planting scheme.

Defining terms

Strictly speaking, a climber is any plant that has adapted to growing through other plants, over banks or up gulleys and rocky outcrops. With twining stems, tendrils, sticky pads, thorns and aerial roots produced along their stems, climbers can cling to vertical surfaces, fasten themselves to cracks and crevices, and haul themselves upwards.

Wall shrubs, on the other hand, form a group of woody, often multi-stemmed plants that can be trained against a wall. This has become such a popular way of growing some hardy shrubs, including pyracantha and flowering quince (*Chaenomeles*), that you rarely see them as freestanding specimens in gardens. Training shrubs vertically up a wall not only shows off their flowers and fruit to perfection, it also helps to overcome their natural tendency to sprawl and look rather untidy. In addition, less-than-hardy shrubs can benefit from being grown against a warm, sheltered wall, allowing you to grow

Pink climbing roses and brilliant blue solanum look fantastic together. Make the most of any vertical space by creating your own climbing combinations.

a greater range of plants outdoors than might otherwise be possible in your garden. Some very hardy shrubs, such as cotoneaster, are really tough and perfect for training up cold and shady north-facing walls where very little else will thrive.

Adding value

There is a huge choice of varieties available, so you'll be able to find at least one climber or wall shrub that will suit any position you have in mind. Climbers are valuable because they can reach up high and grow in awkward spots that other plants

cannot reach, increasing the range of plants that you can grow. Best of all, climbers bring colour, texture and fragrance up to eye level, where they can be best appreciated.

Use climbers to add height, colour and interest to your garden, to tie your planting scheme together, and to introduce strong vertical accents. Some climbers can be used to scramble through established shrubs and trees, extending the period of interest or increasing the impact of a display. Others will sprawl across the ground to cover areas where it's tricky to grow anything at all.

How climbers climb

Nature's great opportunists, climbers have developed a variety of cunning ways to hitch a lift on the nearest upwardly mobile surface, structure or plant so that they can get their leaves into the sun, show off their flowers and scatter their seeds far and wide. Once you understand how each type of climber climbs, you can give those that you choose for your garden the appropriate support. You will also be able to pick the right sort climber for the job when it's impractical to provide any support – for example on a large expanse of wall.

Climbing myths

DAMAGE TO WALLS

It is a common misconception that climbers will damage walls. Provided the wall is in good order before it is clothed with a climber, the layer of foliage will help protect the wall from the elements. However, if the mortar in brick or block walls is soft and crumbly, planting self-clinging climbers such as ivies and climbing hydrangea (*Hydrangea anomala* subsp. *petiolaris*) will exacerbate the problem. Vigorous climbers such as vines and creepers can also be troublesome around windows. Try not to allow them to grow up onto the roof, where they can damage tiles and soffit boards.

DAMAGE TO FOUNDATIONS

Most climbers planted next to house walls won't do any damage. However, if your home is on clay soil, which tends to shrink when dry, avoid planting very vigorous climbers and wall shrubs here as these draw lots of water from the ground when in full leaf.

DAMAGE TO TREES

While not, strictly speaking, a parasite, ivy left unchecked can eventually kill trees by smothering them and robbing them of light. Poorly growing trees can become overwhelmed by a highly vigorous climber, so it is essential to match the vigour of the climber to its host tree or shrub.

Stick-on climbers

These so-called 'self-supporting' climbers hold on by themselves, although they still need a host plant, a vertical surface or a handy structure to scramble up. Some achieve this by producing little aerial roots along their stems, called adventitious roots, which find their way into the smallest cracks and crevices, including the textured surface of stone and brick or the bark of a tree. Ivy is a

Hang a curtain of foliage over walls and fences using self-clinging Boston ivy (*Parthenocissus tricuspidata*).

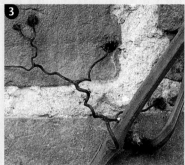

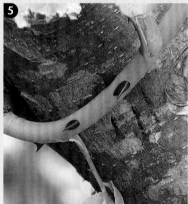

Climbers have developed an impressive range of techniques to get a leg-up on vertical surfaces or neighbouring plants. How they climb will determine the best supports to use.

① Runner beans use their stems to hold on to canes, poles and wigwams.

② Twisting tendrils help climbers such as passion flower to get up high.

③ Virginia creeper and Boston ivy use sticky pads to attach themselves to any surface.

④ Climbing hydrangeas produce aerial roots along their stems that hold on tight.

⑤ Lazy climbers, like this rambler rose, throw up thorny arching stems that hook themselves onto their supports.

classic example of a plant that has got this climbing technique down to a fine art. Other plants, such as Virginia creeper (*Parthenocissus quinquefolia*), have evolved alien-looking tendrils with sticky pads on the end. These reach out and cement the climber to the nearest vertical surface. No cracks or crevices are required, as these pads can attach themselves to painted window frames, glazed tiles and even clean glass.

Twisting climbers

In the garden, twining climbers generally need an artificial support, such as wires attached to a wall or a trellis, so that they can gain a secure purchase up vertical surfaces. Twining climbers don't all spiral in the same direction, however. Many, such as honeysuckle, go round clockwise, while Chinese wisteria (*Wisteria sinensis*) spirals in an anti-clockwise direction. Some climbers don't spiral with their main stem but, like clematis, use modified leaf-stalks. Others, such as the passion flower (*Passiflora*), produce tendrils that curl around and hold on to their host for support. These plants often make very good companion climbers because the leaf-stalks and tendrils don't damage the host plant.

Lazy climbers

Lastly, there are climbers that do not hold on at all, but simply throw up long, whippy, usually arching stems – often with talon-like thorns – that intermingle with a host plant rather than attaching themselves to it. Rambler roses and winter jasmine (*Jasminum nudiflorum*) are good examples of this type of climber and they definitely need wires or a trellis for support, as well as regular tying in as they grow, in order to remain secure. Alternatively, these 'lazy' climbers will make sprawling heaps without support and can be used to cover banks and eyesores as well as providing good ground cover.

Using climbers and wall shrubs

Climbers and wall shrubs offer more growing opportunities than any other group of plants. Choose the right variety and you can cover any vertical or horizontal surface in any position, including the gloomiest north-facing wall. They also have another valuable role – disguising the unsightly.

Verticals and horizontals

A climber trained up an isolated support such as a post or obelisk can be used as a tree substitute to add drama and focus to an otherwise two-dimensional display. This can be particularly useful in a new garden, which needs something to provide instant impact, or in a garden with shallow soil, where larger plants struggle to get established.

Climbers and ground-hugging wall shrubs, such as *Cotoneaster horizontalis*, will usefully cover the soil with weed-smothering foliage, and at the same time form an attractive textured carpet between other permanent plants. A single vigorous specimen can spread far and wide, so this can be an ideal way of covering tricky areas – the inhospitable zone under evergreen trees and shrubs, for example, or a dry, sandy bank – where nothing else will grow.

Softening hard edges

As well as dividing a garden into different areas, climbers and wall shrubs can fill out and soften the geometric outlines of a trellis, as well as breaking up the stark appearance of walls and fences. A climber-clad fence (or 'fedge') is a crafty way of

Don't forget

If you are planning to train soft fruit over an arch, it would be sensible to choose a prickle-free variety, for example the 'Oregon Thornless' blackberry.

Magenta *Lychnis coronaria* enlivens the blues and purples of *Clematis* 'Perle d'Azur' and *Verbena bonariensis*.

A garden divider clad with deep-green ivy creates an intimate seating area with a sense of privacy and seclusion all year round in this overlooked urban garden.

Creating a distraction

To distract your eye from a large eyesore outside the garden or to minimize the impact of less ornamental parts of the garden, such as an ugly garage, you can frame an attractive nearby feature. Canny garden designers use this technique – the framed feature will effectively distract the eye so that the eyesore isn't even noticed. By positioning a series of climber-clad arches down a path, you can force the viewer's gaze down the 'tunnel' you have created to the focal point at the end. Any unattractive features to either side of the walkway will hardly register with the casual observer. On a smaller scale, with something like a large water butt, grow a climbing rose or a clematis over a nearby trellis. Your eye is drawn to the beautiful blooms and diverted away from the water butt.

Create a distraction with colour contrasts, like this perennial golden hop over a brightly stained trellis.

creating the natural outlines of a hedge in a small garden. If you choose carefully, there are climbers that can be used to attract native species of birds and other wildlife by offering shelter, food and nesting sites (*see* page 22). Not all climbers are purely ornamental: several climbing vegetables, such as runner beans with their bright scarlet flowers, not only look pretty but also provide delicious home-grown produce. Fruit trees and bushes can be also be trained to grow up supports, walls and fences.

Camouflage

Many climbers and wall shrubs are relatively quick-growing compared to specimen shrubs, so they're ideal for disguising things you'd rather not look at. If you're trying to hide an old tree stump, try small-leaved ivies, such as the yellow-edged, grey-green leaves of *Hedera helix* 'Goldchild'. Use upright wall shrubs or a screen of climbers to disguise a wheelie-bin area, a compost bin or the roof of an old shed. The bold foliage of a vine will cloak a small shed and provide camouflage.

Light up a shady wall during the summer months with the lacecap flowerheads of the climbing hydrangea.

Soothing blues: *Wisteria floribunda* with a colour-coordinated planting of *Geranium × magnificum*.

The arching stems of the rambler rose 'Albertine' create an informal adornment for a sunny fence.

Walls and fences

Climbers are perfect for creating a backdrop of foliage that will set off any plants in the foreground. Boundary walls and fences that are covered with climbers will blend into their surroundings – and will make the garden seem bigger, too. Nearly any type of climber can be used: roses, clematis, honeysuckle and jasmine are all good choices. Where there is a border in front of the wall or fence, you could select a climber or shrub that puts on just one, dramatic display, with the border plants keeping the show going at other times. However, where there is no opportunity for companion planting, choose a climber or wall shrub, such as a climbing rose or a pyracantha, that will give a long season of interest, especially if the wall or fence is in a prominent position. Whichever climber you choose, make sure it will be happy with the growing conditions and space you have available.

Transforming chain-link

Any chain-link fence can easily be turned into an attractive living 'fedge'. An ivy will give year-round cover, and you'll be able to trim it into a neat, hedge-like feature that provides nesting sites for birds and cover for other wildlife.

Before you start, check the fence is in good condition. Plant the ivy at regular intervals along the fence, initially training it along the bottom wire to ensure complete coverage as quickly as possible. The ivy will produce sideshoots from the leaf-joints of the stem you've tied in and will scamper over the chain-link in just a few years. Once it's covered the fence, clip it with shears. *Hedera colchica* 'Dentata Variegata' is suitable for larger hedges and *Hedera helix* 'Oro di Bogliasco' ('Goldheart') for smaller ones.

Climbing roses

On a standard, shoulder-high panelled fence you can grow all but the most vigorous roses. To achieve the best display, train their shoots into a fan shape so that each stem grows almost parallel with the ground – not only is this pleasing on the eye, it will also encourage better flowering. In stems that are trained horizontally, sap flow is slowed down, encouraging the formation of flower buds rather than extension growth. On a large wall, you have the option to grow the most vigorous roses, but bear in mind they will need training into their support and this will be a lot more difficult if the support is above head height. It's also a good idea to choose disease-resistant roses, such as 'Compassion', when growing them against walls and fences. The air circulation is often restricted in such positions, making it easier for diseases to take hold (*see* page 70).

Arches and pergolas

Arches and pergolas are a popular way of displaying climbers. Arches are more versatile because they can

A simple pergola clothed with leafy climbers will create an intimate corner where you can take time out to relax or eat alfresco with family and friends.

be accommodated in almost any size of garden. They can frame an entrance, a seat or a focal point. They can also act as dividers between one part of the garden and the next. Both arches and pergolas provide extra shelter from the sun or wind in exposed situations, and they are a good way of creating privacy in an overlooked garden. Arches can also create the illusion that a small garden is larger than it really is.

Generally speaking, arches can accommodate smaller, less vigorous climbers, while well-constructed pergolas should be ideal for almost any size of climber. However, to make training easier choose climbers with pliable stems such as clematis or jasmine. And it goes without saying that thorny climbers on narrow arches are not a good idea.

Scented arches

Fragrance is an important consideration when choosing climbers for arches. Roses are firm favourites and – perfect for those narrow arches – there are some virtually thornless varieties: *Rosa* 'Zéphirine Drouhin' (deep-pink, late-summer flowers) and the more modern 'Generous Gardener' (double, pale pink, summer flowers) are both good choices. Honey-scented honeysuckles, such as *Lonicera periclymenum* 'Belgica' (purple and yellow flowers from late spring) or 'Serotina' (creamy-white and deep-pink, summer flowers), will add charm to any archway, looking particularly at home in cottage-garden plantings. For a sturdy arch in a hot, sunny spot a wisteria would be an ideal choice.

Quick cover-up

When you plant climbers to grow in prominent places, such as up arches and over pergolas, they can look rather stark and unattractive for the first few seasons while they're getting established and filling out. A great way of improving their appearance in the early years is to plant some annual climbers alongside them to beef up the display. Excellent annuals that fit the bill include the cup-and-saucer vine (*Cobaea scandens*), morning glory (*Ipomoea tricolor*), sweet peas (*Lathyrus odoratus*), black-eyed Susan (*Thunbergia alata*) and canary creeper (*Tropaeolum peregrinum*).

The owner of this small garden has made the most of every available vertical space by growing a wide range of climbers for colour and interest.

A stunning clematis scrambling up a tripod in a glazed pot provides a mobile focal point within a garden.

Climbers for patios

Some climbers look at home alongside walls and paving, breaking up hard lines and softening edges with a frill of flowers and foliage. The bricks and slabs will also act like night-storage heaters, keeping the immediate area around the plants warm at night and enabling you to extend your options to include less hardy climbers. Try the fast-growing Chilean glory flower (*Eccremocarpus scaber*), which throws out exotic-looking spikes of orange-red, tubular blooms all summer long, or the flame creeper (*Tropaeolum speciosum*), with long-spurred, flaming-red flowers produced from midsummer onwards.

Many climbers can also be grown successfully in containers on the patio. Choose a container at least 45cm (18in) deep and wide. Free-flowering compact forms of clematis can look especially spectacular in pots. For early flowers try one of the varieties of *Clematis alpina* or *Clematis macropetala*, and choose a large-flowered hybrid for a summer display. (*See also* page 40.)

Adding height to borders

One of the easiest ways of improving an existing garden with climbers is to add height to pancake-flat displays. By training a climber up a simple post you instantly add a point of focus as well as introducing variation in height. In addition, the viewer's eye has to pause at this point and this will bring the rest of the border into view. A climber growing up a metal or wooden obelisk will also provide seasonal variation and can be chosen to extend and increase the impact of the existing colour scheme.

You can create focal points that change according to the time of year by choosing the right climbers. A winter jasmine (*Jasminum nudiflorum*), for example, may look inconspicuous for much of the year but becomes the centre of attention during the coldest months, when its glowing yellow flowers shine out from the gloom.

The interlacing stems and indigo-blue flowers of *Clematis × durandii* weave their magic through a purple-themed border filled with lupins, roses and delphiniums.

Late-flowering *Clematis* 'Warszawka Nike' offers height and rich colour even where space is at a premium.

Climbers as ground cover

Many climbers are happy scrambling across the ground and they grow and flower just as well in this position as they do growing up a support. Climbers make an interesting and unusual ground-cover option between permanent plants anywhere in the garden: their long, trailing stems allow them to cover ground where little else will grow. Use shade-loving climbers, such as ivies, to weave a green carpet under evergreen shrubs or along the base on the shady side of an evergreen hedge. On the other hand, sun-loving wall shrubs such as the low-growing ceanothus, *Ceanothus thyrsiflorus* var. *repens*, will cloak a sun-baked bank that would be too hot for other ground-cover plants. Banks that remain moist are a particularly good way of showing off clematis on the flat. You could try combining a clematis with an evergreen ivy to provide year-round cover that will also act as an effective weed suppressor.

Bear in mind that climbers can be grown horizontally anywhere in the garden. Between well-spaced permanent deciduous trees and shrubs you can try really vigorous climbers such as the large-leaved Persian ivy (*Hedera colchica*), paired with a quick-growing clematis such as *Clematis montana*. Or try a honeysuckle, such as *Lonicera periclymenum*, that enjoys dappled shade. It is important to match the vigour of the climber to the ground area you wish to cover, so if the permanent plants are more closely spaced choose climbers that won't grow too large. Underplanting with spring- and autumn-flowering bulbs will help extend the flowering season and keep the ground cover looking attractive for longer.

Give an entrance maximum impact with the sun-loving wall shrub *Fremontodendron californicum*, which will appreciate being sheltered from cold winds.

Framing an entrance

One of the most important areas for climbers and wall shrubs is next to the door of your house or your garden gate. It's best to choose

A carpet of ivy provides the perfect foil for the striking bark of this multi-stemmed Chinese red birch.

plants that complement the style of your entrance, as well as being happy growing in the conditions there. On a sheltered, sunny site, you could try the white forsythia (*Abeliophyllum distichum*), which has pretty, star-shaped flowers in spring that are also sweetly scented. Or you could train an evergreen ceanothus, such as *Ceanothus* 'Concha', up the wall next to your doorway. The dark, glossy foliage will provide interest all year round, and in late spring the fluffy blooms of richest, deep blue will look terrific against a brick wall, stonework or white render.

Don't forget

For a permanent planting by an entrance, choose a climber that isn't too vigorous and offers interest for much of the year. And remember to improve the soil before planting, to help it get established (see pages 44–5).

For entrances with an east- or west-facing aspect, you could try the rather exotic-looking *Billardiera longiflora*. After the greenish flowers have faded, it produces eye-catching deep-purple, red, pink or white, miniature pepper-shaped fruit. If your doorway or gate is in a rather exposed situation, try a clematis such as 'Comtesse de Bouchaud' (rose-pink flowers), 'Ernest Markham' (velvety-red flowers) or 'Lasurstern' (sky-blue flowers). Honeysuckles will also work well here: *Lonicera* 'Dropmore Scarlet' is good value with flaming-scarlet, tubular flowers that are often followed by red berries in warm summers. For the more challenging, northerly aspects, your choice might include *Garrya elliptica*, the climbing hydrangea (*Hydrangea anomala* subsp. *petiolaris*), a jasmine or a pyracantha (*see* page 108).

Take care when choosing plants for fragrance because scents are perceived very differently by different people. What one person may consider delightful can seem rather insipid or even sickly to another. Before planting any scented climber get right up close and personal with it to make sure it's right for you.

Sniff fragrant flowers in bloom before you buy to make sure you like the scent.
① Honeysuckles are among the most fragrant of climbing plants.
② Scented climbers are especially appreciated when trained around a seating area.
③ Fragrant, evergreen star jasmine smells delicious in a warm, sheltered spot.

Scented climbers

With natural charm and romantic associations, roses, jasmines and honeysuckles are often top of the list for providing heady fragrance. When choosing a scented rose, however, avoid the most vigorous varieties unless you have the space. Also, opt for roses with pliable stems – they are easier to train. A well-behaved rambling rose such as 'Emily Gray' is a safe bet and will look good all year. You can extend the scented season by adding fragrant climbers that bloom at different times. During spring the evergreen *Clematis* 'Apple Blossom' is smothered in lovely almond-scented, star-shaped, creamy blooms and then, in early summer, *Clematis* 'Elizabeth' comes into its own, bearing fragrant, yellow-centred, soft-pink flowers. And the star jasmine (*Trachelospermum jasminoides*) is a terrific evergreen climber that bears lovely clusters of jasmine-scented, starry white flowers from midsummer onwards – but you must give it a sunny, sheltered spot.

Fragrant seating areas

One of the most charming features you can create, even in the smallest garden, is a secluded fragrant seat. Start with a garden bench and put up a wooden arch or a mini-pergola over it, to support your choice of climbers. Fill in the back with a decorative trellis. The seat should be located in a warm spot that catches sun for at least part of the day, perhaps late afternoon, and well away from prying eyes. Avoid very sunny corners unless you enjoy being baked on a hot day and, most importantly, make sure your seat has an attractive outlook.

Creative effects and uses

Climbers and wall shrubs open up many interesting design options, allowing you to add that personal touch that sets your garden apart from others. The strong vertical or horizontal lines of trained plants can introduce drama, while foliage and flowers soften edges and introduce lovely organic shapes.

Create a striking arbour around an elegant garden bench by framing it with a rose-clad arch, backed by a leafy trellis covered with a yellow-green golden hop.

Climbers and wall shrubs can be used as the 'glue' that holds the different elements of a garden design together. They have the ability to link diverse features in the garden, weaving them into a coherent whole by means of natural, sweeping curves, colourful flowers and textural foliage. A good way of linking adjacent beds and borders is to plant climbers over a connecting arch, or drape them along ropes between posts at the back of a border to create a spectacular coordinated backdrop.

Grouping supports

A series of posts, obelisks or tripods with climbers scrambling up them can have a dramatic impact in parallel borders either side of a path. The further from the path the posts are positioned, the less they will be noticed – but they will actually make the garden seem bigger. Vertical supports can reinforce and emphasize existing patterns: set them in a straight line to enhance a formal scheme or group them more loosely if they follow the arc of a curving border. You can use supports like sentries at the end of the borders, or set them right next to the edge of a path. Choose modern, repeat-flowering, trouble-free roses to climb up them, such as 'Aloha' (double, rose-pink and salmon flowers) or 'Bantry Bay' (deep rose-pink flowers).

Enhancing focal points

Climbers, as we have seen, are sometimes used to distract the eye or provide camouflage, but they can also be used to draw the eye. You can double the impact of an existing feature, either within or outside the garden, by framing it with a climber. A climber-clad arch over a sundial at the end of a vista, for example, will be so magnetic to the eye that little else around it will be noticed. Alternatively, you could frame a feature beyond the garden, such as an impressive view or a distant church steeple so that it stands out like a picture on a wall. Bear in mind the scale of the feature and match the climber and its support to it – like choosing the right frame for a picture. Large-leaved climbers, for example, look best framing chunky focal points such as sundials or pieces of sculpture, while small-leaved climbers suit features that are viewed at close quarters. Colour is important, too. If the main attraction of the feature you want to bring into focus is its colour, choose a climber of a complementary or contrasting shade.

Turn a favourite garden ornament into a dynamic focal point by framing it with a climber-covered arch, here enhanced by the azure flowers of clematis.

Garlands of colour and fragrance – the scented rambling rose 'Kiftsgate' paired with *Clematis* 'Prince Charles'.

Posts and colonnades

To achieve extra height, consider growing climbers over a purpose-built framework of sturdy posts linked with crossbars and strengthened with cross-pieces. Or for an informal effect, make a colonnade with looped ropes and wooden posts. Both clematis and roses with pliable stems lend themselves to training in this way, but roses are the traditional option. (*See also* page 110.)

Climber-clad walkways

Covered walkways can make very attractive features. They are available in kit form, which can prove expensive, or you could construct your own using an inexpensive series of arches spaced along a garden path. If you have a sizeable plot consider a large, climber-clad pergola – an impressive structure that could provide a shady refuge down one side of a sunny, south-facing garden.

Climbers and wall shrubs for wildlife

Climbers and wall shrubs that clothe walls and fences in a thick layer of stems and foliage provide the perfect cover for a variety of wild creatures. Some even offer nesting sites for small, native birds and provide vital food sources throughout the year.

Tall wall shrubs that have branching stems clothed in evergreen foliage, such as pyracanthas, make good nesting sites. Train them against a wall or fence, grow them up a garden building, or plant them as part of a hedge in sun or shade. Overgrown honeysuckles with a mass of woody stems, out of the reach of predators, are also prime real estate among the feathered community. To improve the chances of birds nesting in your climbers, install nesting boxes that are well hidden in the stems and foliage.

Berrying climbers

The most useful plants for birds are those with berries carried throughout winter. Oriental bittersweet (*Celastrus orbiculatus*) is a good choice, producing decorative yellow seed capsules that split to reveal glistening pink and scarlet fruits in autumn. The scarlet, bead-like fruits of herringbone cotoneaster (*Cotoneaster horizontalis*) also provide nourishment in the winter. Only if you have a huge amount of space or a really large, mature tree to support its weight, consider the beautiful but rampant rambler *Rosa filipes* 'Kiftsgate', whose blooms will attract pollinating insects and are followed by glossy red hips.

Ivy, which produces yellowish-green flowers then spherical black fruits, is an

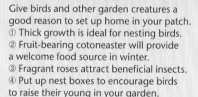

Give birds and other garden creatures a good reason to set up home in your patch.
① Thick growth is ideal for nesting birds.
② Fruit-bearing cotoneaster will provide a welcome food source in winter.
③ Fragrant roses attract beneficial insects.
④ Put up nest boxes to encourage birds to raise their young in your garden.

excellent choice for wildlife gardens, because it offers food and nesting sites for many native bird species, including the wren. Honeysuckles, too, are ideal climbers for planting in a dedicated wildlife area. *Lonicera japonica* var. *repens,* which has fragrant flowers followed by small, purple-black fruits, is a reliable variety.

Seasonal maintenance

Make sure any young birds have flown the nest before you begin cutting back climbers and wall shrubs, and don't thin out congested growth too much. It may be better to carry out any necessary pruning during the winter. To get the best crop of berries on wall shrubs, such as pyracanthas, prune carefully as soon as the flowers have faded, so that you leave as many fruiting spurs as possible.

Edible climbers and wall plants

Sunny walls, fences, arches and pergolas are ideal places to grow edible climbers, including grapevines. You can also train bush fruits that tolerate cooler conditions – gooseberries and currants, perhaps – against east- and west-facing walls and fences, where there is direct sun for only part of the day.

Squeeze fruit and vegetables into a small space by growing them vertically.
① Fruit bushes, like this whitecurrant, can be trained along wires up a wall.
② In a vegetable garden, try growing a squash over an improvised arch.

Blackberries have long, pliable stems that are perfect for training up supports, over arches or along fences and wires, and raspberries can be trained up canes to create vertical accents and edible garden dividers, too. Trained fruit trees, although not strictly wall shrubs, will also appreciate the extra sunlight, warmth and shelter that a south-facing wall or fence provides. Unless you buy ready-trained fruit trees, which are very expensive, you will have to do much of the training yourself. There are three basic training methods to choose from: cordon, fan or espalier. Espaliers are arguably the most decorative form, with equally spaced, horizontal tiers of branches on either side of an upright main stem. Smaller versions, with a knee-high single tier on a stumpy stem, are called stepovers.

Climbing vegetables

A few vegetables lend themselves to covering fences, walls and other structures, such as arches. Runner beans are perhaps the most obvious, not only because they are naturally strong climbers, but because they look so decorative in flower. Harvesting doesn't detract from their ornamental appeal; indeed, it promotes continued flower production. Runner beans are also ideal for covering an arch leading to a fruit or vegetable garden. Similarly, climbing French beans can be trained to cover vertical surfaces. Although the flowers are less decorative than the scarlet blooms of runner beans, some have attractively coloured pods, ranging from yellow and red to purple. There are also multi-coloured varieties. If they are not harvested until the end of the season, 'haricot' varieties can be

used dry. Grow them up a wigwam of canes to create height in a border.

Don't overlook squashes and even cucumbers for growing as ornamental climbers. Their flowers and fruit are really attractive, especially the smaller-fruited and brightly coloured varieties. Combining climbing vegetables with annual flowering climbers, such as sweet peas, doubles the decorative effect and gives you extra produce for the kitchen as well as flowers for the table.

Climbing vegetables

Runner beans – 'Lady Di', 'Painted Lady', 'Red Knight', 'Sunset'

French beans – 'Borlotto Lingua di Fuoco', 'Corona d'Orso', 'Purple Queen', 'Purple Teepee'

Squashes – 'Custard Apple', 'Sweet Dumpling', 'White Patty Pan'

Growing climbers with other plants

Some climbers have a spectacular but all-too-fleeting flowering season. If the weather is wet and windy, the flowers can be over before you've even noticed them. Growing climbers through established trees and shrubs, as well as pairing them with each other, will ensure maximum impact.

Growing into trees, shrubs and hedges

In the wild, climbers' natural supports are other plants, in particular trees and large shrubs. In your garden, planting climbers to grow through trees and shrubs is an excellent way of showing them off to their best advantage. But make sure you choose the right climber so that the host plant doesn't get swamped. Some trees make better hosts than others: trees that have an open canopy allow dappled sunlight to filter through. Mountain ash, silver birch and fruit trees such as apples and pears are the most accommodating. Large, tree-like shrubs, such as magnolias, lilacs, holly and hawthorn, also make good host plants, as do evergreens such as Lawson cypress.

How to plant

Plant your climber carefully, well away from the host plant so that it can become established and is not shaded out. Generally, the soil around a tree will be drier than elsewhere, partly because the tree roots remove large quantities of moisture, but also because the canopy of the tree produces a rain-shadow effect, with a 'drip zone' running around the edge of the canopy. This zone is the best position for new twining and scrambling climbers, such as roses, since water will get right down to their roots, where it's needed. On exposed sites, plant on the windward side of the tree, so that the climber is blown into its host rather than away from it, enabling it to take advantage of wind-blown rain. Then

Hebe 'Watson's Pink' offers good support to *Clematis* 'Prince Charles', and the pretty pink and mauve flower tones make a harmonious blend.

train it up into the canopy along a staked rope or chain, with the other end attached to a stout branch; use a special tree tie that won't strangle or cut into the branch. This method of training a climber into a tree will prevent the natural swaying of the host plant from ripping the climber out of the ground.

Don't forget

When choosing a climber to grow into an established shrub, tree or hedge, you need to take into account the flowering time to make the most of the partnership. You can either choose a climber that flowers at the same time as the host plant to double the impact of the display, or choose one that flowers at a different time to spread the period of interest.

For a really dramatic contrast grow wisteria through a mature laburnum tree. This bold pairing brings out the vibrancy of both colours.

Climbers to try in trees, shrubs and hedges

Celastrus orbiculatus (oriental bittersweet) – The scalloped leaves of this twining climber turn yellow in autumn and are followed by huge clusters of scarlet autumn fruits. Good with large trees.

Clematis alpina (alpine clematis) – The tiny, nodding, bell-shaped, blue flowers with creamy centres bloom from spring to early summer, followed by fluffy seedheads. Good with large shrubs, such as philadelphus and hawthorn.

Clematis 'Comtesse de Bouchaud' – In mid- to late summer this clematis is covered in yellow-centred, mauve-pink flowers. Good with medium-sized evergreen conifers and hedges.

Clematis 'Elizabeth' – Fragrant, yellow-centred, soft-pink flowers appear in late spring and early summer. Good with smaller trees such as mountain ash and holly.

Clematis 'Jackmanii Superba' – The mid- to late-summer flowers are a lovely, velvety purple. Good with small trees such as mountain ash and laburnum.

Fallopia baldschuanica (Russian vine) – A very vigorous climber, it is smothered in sprays of tiny, funnel-shaped, pink-flushed white flowers during late summer. Good with very large evergreens, such as Leyland cypress.

Hedera colchica 'Sulphur Heart' – This Persian ivy's evergreen leaves with creamy-yellow splodges are heart-shaped. Good with large trees such as ash, beech and sycamore.

Hedera helix 'Glacier' – The evergreen, grey-green leaves of this English ivy are decorated with silver-grey and cream markings. Good with small or medium-sized trees.

Humulus lupulus 'Aureus' (golden hop) – This beautiful hop is covered with vine-like, yellow-green, deciduous leaves. Good with medium-sized, purple-leaved shrubs, such as *Sambucus nigra*, or medium-sized trees such as *Prunus cerasifera* 'Nigra'.

Hydrangea anomala subsp. *petiolaris* (climbing hydrangea) – Suitable for shady areas, this bears delicate, creamy-white, lacecap flowers in late spring and early summer. Good with large trees.

Lathyrus latifolius (everlasting pea) – A succession of fragrant, pinkish-purple, sweet-pea-like blooms are produced from summer to early autumn. Good with small trees, such as magnolia, as well as fruit trees.

Rosa 'Albéric Barbier' – Sprays of double, slightly scented, creamy flowers bloom in early summer and again in late summer. Good with small trees such as apples, pears, holly, lilac and laburnum.

Rosa filipes 'Kiftsgate' – Single, fragrant, creamy-coloured flowers are borne throughout late summer and early autumn followed by glossy red hips. A really rampant rambler, it is good with any really large, mature tree.

Rosa 'Wedding Day' – Clusters of fragrant, creamy-coloured flowers bloom in summer. Good with medium-sized trees such as *Prunus cerasifera* 'Nigra'.

Tropaeolum speciosum (flame creeper) – The long-spurred, flaming-red flowers bloom from midsummer into early autumn. Good with evergreen hedges with dark foliage (*see* right).

For most of the climbers listed above, *see* pages 73–105.

A richly coloured clematis threading its way through leafy branches will add interest and impact to any tree.

Liven up an expanse of yew hedge by growing the vibrant-coloured flame creeper (*Tropaeolum speciosum*) through it.

Effortless elegance – the purple and plum of two exquisite clematis, 'Viola' and 'Emilia Plater', stand out against a white backdrop in this classic planting.

large-flowered hybrids will perform doubly well because they will appreciate the extra shelter and support the evergreen offers. With a clematis in flower every month of the year, it won't be hard to choose one that will bloom to fit in with your existing climbers or wall shrubs. You could grow 'The President', which flowers in early to midsummer, to fill the gap between flowers and berries on a pyracantha. Or combine a clematis that flowers in spring, such as *Clematis armandii*, with a repeat-flowering climbing rose. The clematis will be over before the rose comes into bloom but its glossy evergreen foliage remains. For a striking display, try growing the large, semi-double, yellow *Rosa* 'Golden Showers' with the creamy-centred, deep-purple flowers of *Clematis* 'Etoile Violette'. If you're unsure about combining colours, go for a fail-safe partnership such as a pale pink rose – perhaps 'New Dawn' – with your favourite clematis, and for maximum impact choose one that has a hint of white in the flower.

Companionable clematis

Clematis combine especially well with many other climbers, including honeysuckles, roses and ivies, as well as with wall shrubs. If you're trying to improve an existing display, it's always a good idea to start with clematis. Particularly useful for disguising the gnarled stems of well-established woody climbers such as wisteria and roses, clematis are equally at home growing alongside flowering quinces (*Chaenomeles*) and through pyracanthas and ceanothus. Paired with an evergreen shrub, many

Don't forget

Try to match the vigour of the clematis to that of its climbing partner or wall shrub. For example, the more vigorous varieties of *Clematis montana* and *Clematis tangutica* will quickly overwhelm any slow-growing companions. Similarly, it's a mismatch to train a compact, well-behaved clematis through an extremely rampant climber such as Russian vine (*Fallopia baldschuanica*).

Good companions

Combine climbers with each other or with other plants to bring out the best of both, or to extend the season of interest.

① Let the small-flowered *Clematis viticella* – covered with pixy-hat-shaped blooms from midsummer until early autumn – weave itself through the foliage of ground-hugging winter-flowering heathers to make a long-lasting display.

② The ruby red of the clematis 'Niobe' and the rich pink, delightfully fragrant blooms of the climbing rose 'Zéphirine Drouhin' are perfectly harmonious in sun or semi-shade.

③ Extend the rich crimson-red tones from summer into autumn by pairing a Virginia creeper that will turn a brilliant red with the lily-flowered clematis 'Gravetye Beauty'.

④ Add year-round interest with the evergreen partnership of *Clematis armandii* and variegated ivy (*Hedera helix*). The display peaks during early spring when the clematis is smothered in almond-scented, creamy-white flowers.

OTHER GOOD COMPANIONS

Clematis 'Comtesse de Bouchaud' (soft mauve-pink flowers) is the perfect partner for *Hydrangea anomala* subsp. *petiolaris* (loose, white lacecap flowers). When the hydrangea has finished flowering, the cool pink clematis blooms shine out from the hydrangea's dark foliage.

Eccremocarpus scaber (dramatic, orange-red flowers) works well with *Clematis tangutica* (yellow, bell-shaped flowers) if you want a bold, exotic-looking summer display.

Humulus lupulus 'Aureus' (golden-yellow leaves) provides a curtain of bright foliage from spring onwards, making a wonderful backdrop for the contrasting blooms of *Clematis* 'Etoile Violette' (rich, velvety-looking purple flowers).

Wisteria sinensis (shades of blue to violet) and *Rosa* 'New Dawn' (double, pearly-pink flowers) make a lovely, fragrant pairing. The wisteria's perfume will fill the air in early summer; later, the scent of the rose takes over.

Synchronizing pruning

When combining clematis with other plants, it's important to bear in mind the pruning requirements of your clematis to make routine maintenance as easy as possible (*see* pages 78, 83–4). To go with a repeat-flowering climbing rose or with wall shrubs, choose a clematis that requires little or no pruning, but with a rambler rose that needs cutting back hard, go for a clematis that also needs hard pruning during late winter or early spring.

Clematis also combine beautifully with each other. Again, it is a good idea to synchronize their pruning requirements to make life easier for yourself. Choose clematis varieties from the same pruning group, but with slightly different flowering times (and maybe different colours), so that you achieve a continuous flowering display over a long period.

Many tender climbers make wonderful conservatory plants. Some are ideal for covering expanses of wall; others can be used like natural blinds to scramble through the roof supports of a sun-drenched conservatory or greenhouse. More exotic plants, on the other hand, need hot rooms indoors to thrive. There are several frost-tender climbers that cannot cope with winter wet or bitingly cold winds and should be grown in pots in a sunny spot, and brought indoors to overwinter.

Brighten up unheated indoor spaces with these stylish climbers.
① Grown indoors and pruned correctly, vines will bear fruit.
② Cape leadwort (*Plumbago auriculata*) produces exquisite sky-blue flowers.

Climbers for cold rooms
(minimum -5°C/23°F)

If you have an unheated conservatory and it is on the spacious side, plant a grapevine such as *Vitis vinifera* 'Schiava Grossa'. It will instantly create a Mediterranean feel as well as supplying a crop of edible fruits. Give this vine a raised bed for sufficient root space, or plant it just outside the greenhouse or conservatory and train it in through a specially prepared opening. Add a touch of the tropics to your space with the eye-catching climber *Clianthus puniceus*, which bears lipstick-red, lobster-claw blooms from spring to early summer. The half-hardy white potato vine (*Solanum laxum* 'Album') or the blue passion flower (*Passiflora caerulea*) are ideal for large containers in an unheated conservatory.

Climbers for cool rooms
(minimum 0°C/32°F)

In a greenhouse or conservatory kept just frost free during the winter

months, add a splash of summer and autumn colour with a bougainvillea, such as the sugar-pink 'Tango'. For a longer period of interest, consider the yellow and green variegated foliage of 'Tropical Rainbow', which also bears cerise-coloured flowers. Evergreen

Cape leadwort (*Plumbago auriculata*) is a lovely plant for an indoor display, especially from summer to late autumn when it's smothered in sky-blue flowers. A frost-free environment also allows you to grow the pretty, evergreen bluebell creeper (*Sollya heterophylla*), which will thrive in bright, filtered light, as well as the frost-tender, deliciously fragrant common jasmine (*Jasminum officinale*).

Climbers for warm rooms
(minimum 5°C/41°F)

An indoor room kept slightly warm allows you to grow a few choice but tender varieties of flowering climbers. Although most passion flowers can cope with a touch of frost, the firm favourite *Passiflora* 'Amethyst' needs slightly more protection during the coldest months to guarantee survival.

① *Mandevilla* × *amoena* 'Alice du Pont' has glowing pink flowers.
② For night-time perfume grow the wax plant (*Hoya carnosa*).
③ This indoor bower is packed with exotic-looking climbers that will thrive given year-round warmth.

Similarly, the wax plant (*Hoya carnosa*) is a little gem that is worth growing for its dense clusters of night-scented, white or pink flowers from late spring until autumn.

Climbers for hot rooms
(minimum 15°C/59°F)

Where the temperature is kept high all year round, you can grow a range of exotics such as the fragrant white bridal wreath (*Stephanotis floribunda*) or the twining evergreen glory bower (*Clerodendrum thomsoniae*), which produces cascading clusters of white and crimson bell-shaped flowers throughout summer. The woody-stemmed climber *Mandevilla* is also fairly spectacular, especially *Mandevilla splendens*, which has huge 10cm (4in) rose-pink, trumpet-shaped blooms.

Caring for indoor climbers: the practicalities

■ Most plants need to be kept out of the midday sun, so some form of shading may be required in a south-facing greenhouse or conservatory during the summer. Keep temperatures below 26°C (79°F) using shading, ventilation, misting and even damping down if necessary.

■ Grow most climbers and wall shrubs in containers filled with a loam-based compost, such as John Innes No. 2, but for more vigorous climbers, such as passion flowers, opt for the richer John Innes No. 3.

■ Water as necessary during the growing season and feed monthly using a balanced liquid fertilizer, or incorporate a slow-release fertilizer at planting time and then reapply each spring.

■ Keep the atmosphere moist around tropical climbers using a hand-mister and stand smaller plants on trays of damp gravel to maintain high humidity. Water sparingly during the winter months.

■ Top-dress all permanent plants each spring by replacing the top few centimetres of compost with fresh, or repot if necessary.

■ Watch out for pests and diseases and take appropriate action as soon as you notice any symptoms or pests (*see* pages 68–71). Whitefly, spider mite and mealy bugs are all fairly common problems with conservatory plants.

Using colour

Colour brings out an emotional response, which is highly individual, so selecting the right colours for your garden is a very personal choice. Colour is closely linked to mood and atmosphere, from soft, romantic and relaxing to vibrant, exciting and dramatic.

You could argue that as gardens have become consistently smaller over recent years, climbers and wall shrubs have become a more important feature within them. In limited spaces, boundary walls and fences are particularly significant elements and, of course, vertical planting is very economical on garden space. So, your choice of colours for your climbers and wall shrubs is key to setting the tone and style of your garden. In addition, limiting the range of colours in your design is a good way of defining the mood you're trying to create.

Transform a shady wall or fence into a bright focal point with the zingy, yellow-green foliage of the golden hop (*Humulus lupulus* 'Aureus').

Understated and stylish, the white garden at Sissinghurst is a calm oasis. If you are experimenting with colour, remember that less is often more.

Grow *Clematis × durandii* near a seating area so the indigo-blue flowers form a relaxing backdrop.

The bell-shaped flowers and fresh green foliage of *Clematis macropetala* look charming in large containers.

This morning glory has stunning blue flowers – little wonder that it is named *Ipomoea* 'Heavenly Blue'.

Cool blues

Calm and soothing, blue is from the 'cool' side of the spectrum, bringing a restful and contemplative air to a planting scheme. Blues are very accommodating colours: they work well with yellow in spring schemes, with rich reds in early summer, and even complement contrasting colours, such as lime green. Bear in mind that the perception of blues, in particular, changes as light levels fluctuate, so a plant that might look dramatic at the beginning or the end of the day may be completely inconspicuous at other times. Blues are at their best in dappled light; in direct sun they can look purple or even mauve. Add a contrasting shade – perhaps orange – to a predominantly blue border to help maintain definition and structure.

Blue-flowered climbers

The most impressive blue climbers are undoubtedly clematis. 'Francis Rivis' is an early bloomer, carrying nodding, bell-shaped, powder-blue flowers from spring to early summer. On a north-facing wall or fence you could opt for the cream-centred, deep-blue flowers of *Clematis macropetala* 'Lagoon'. By early summer *Clematis* 'Blue Eyes', with its lovely sky-blue flowers, takes centre stage, and in late summer 'Perle d'Azur' comes into its own. If you are looking for an unusual climber for a pot on the patio, try the bluebell creeper (*Sollya heterophylla*), which produces a succession of tiny, pendent, blue bells all summer, followed by blue berries.

Blue wall shrubs

Perhaps the best blue wall shrubs can be found among the California lilacs. Bushy *Ceanothus × delileanus* 'Gloire de Versailles' is one of the hardiest and is smothered in powder-blue flower clusters from midsummer to autumn. If you have a sheltered wall or fence, try the slightly less hardy but more intense, spreading evergreen form with attractive, dark green foliage called *Ceanothus* 'Blue Mound'. Its fluffy clusters of deep-blue flowers appear during early summer.

More blue flowers

BLUE CLIMBERS
Clematis alpina 'Pamela Jackman'
Clematis 'Arabella'
Clematis 'Daniel Deronda'
Clematis 'Frankie'
Clematis 'Happy Anniversary'
Clematis 'Helsingborg'
Clematis macropetala 'Wesselton'
Clematis 'Multi Blue'
Wisteria floribunda
Wisteria × formosa
Wisteria sinensis 'Prolific'

BLUE WALL SHRUBS
Ceanothus arboreus 'Trewithen Blue'
Ceanothus 'Autumnal Blue'
Ceanothus 'Burkwoodii'
Ceanothus griseus var. *horizontalis* 'Yankee Point'
Ceanothus thyrsiflorus var. *repens*
Ceanothus thyrsiflorus 'Skylark'
Rosmarinus officinalis

Choose the female form of *Schisandra rubriflora* and you'll enjoy scarlet berries after the flowers.

Darkest red *Rosa* 'Guinée' is a little tricky to grow, but its colour and fragrance are superb.

Grow *Lonicera × brownii* 'Dropmore Scarlet' up a trellis in dappled shade and marvel at its dramatic blooms.

Molten reds and oranges

Fiery shades of red and orange really turn up the temperature of the garden. Not all shades of red have the same impact, however. Scarlet and orange are hot and sultry in a sunny spot and create a sense of drama. Purple-reds, on the other hand, are cooler, becoming darker and more atmospheric – even moody – as the light falters towards the end of the day. Purple, silver and green complement reds but for a really sizzling display team red and orange with rich golds.

Red, red roses

The most sumptuous reds belong to roses and clematis, but the fiery autumn foliage of the creepers and vines comes a close second. To cover a sunny wall on your house or garage consider a brilliant red climbing rose. Some flower twice and many are fragrant. 'Dublin Bay' is a repeat-flowering climber that produces clusters of double red flowers over a long period. When it comes to clematis, 'Gravetye Beauty' is a real stunner, with unusual brilliant crimson, late-summer flowers resembling lily-flowered tulips, while the ruby-red blooms of 'Niobe' make it a popular impulse-buy at the garden centre. Yet the old favourite, 'Ville de Lyon', with its yellow-centred, carmine-red, late-summer flowers is still hard to beat.

Exotic climbers

There are a number of exotic beauties with flaming-red flowers that will add a tropical touch. The trumpet vine *Campsis × tagliabuana* 'Madame Galen' produces fiery orange-red trumpets during late summer, while the coral plant (*Berberidopsis corallina*) carries pendent strings of ruby-red flower clusters on gracefully arching stems. The scarlet trumpet honeysuckle *Lonicera × brownii* 'Dropmore Scarlet' also fits well into exotic schemes. Wall shrubs for mild regions include

More red flowers

RED CLIMBERS

Campsis grandiflora
Campsis radicans 'Flamenco'
Clematis 'Abundance'
Clematis 'Madame Julia Correvon'
Clematis 'Rouge Cardinal'
Rosa 'Altissimo'
Rosa 'American Pillar'
Rosa 'Danse du Feu'
Rosa 'Etoile de Hollande'
Rosa 'Paul's Scarlet Climber'
Tropaeolum majus

RED WALL SHRUBS

Callistemon citrinus 'Splendens'
Camellia japonica 'Adolphe Audusson'
Camellia × williamsii 'Ruby Wedding'
Chaenomeles speciosa 'Simonii'
Chaenomeles × superba 'Crimson and Gold'
Pyracantha 'Mohave'

the trailing abutilon (*Abutilon megapotamicum*) with striking red and yellow flowers. In cooler areas, use it as an unusual patio plant; it can be brought indoors in winter.

Evergreens for year-round interest

Evergreen climbers and wall shrubs can transform boundary walls and fences into living, leafy screens. They also provide valuable texture and structure. Some with handsome foliage, such as variegated ivy, offer year-round interest, while others give spectacular displays of colourful flowers that can be appreciated at head height.

The evergreen year

If you have the space, you can have flowering evergreens in bloom virtually every month of the year. Although many evergreen shrubs are hardy, some are vulnerable to damage from cold winds and most appreciate being grown against a sheltered wall or fence, or given protection in colder regions. Make sure you plant new evergreen shrubs and climbers during late spring, so that they have plenty of time to get established before the onset of their first winter.

Spring

During the spring, camellias appreciate the extra shelter a wall or fence can provide. Most are hardy, but against a sheltered wall you can show off their blooms and help protect them from the worst of the weather. Popular varieties of *Camellia japonica* and *Camellia × williamsii* are ideal for a wall in partial shade, provided it doesn't catch the early morning sun in spring – rapid thawing after a frost can damage the flowers, which will develop unsightly brown patches. Evergreen *Clematis armandii*, with masses of scented, star-shaped blooms, also needs protection from cold winds.

Summer

In a really mild spot, you could try one or two unusual summer-flowering evergreen climbers and wall shrubs

Evergreen climbers add essential form and structure.
① *Clematis armandii* cascades over a pergola – a strong contrast to the clipped box balls.
② *Clematis cirrhosa* var. *purpurascens* scrambles through a pyracantha.

such as the coral plant (*Berberidopsis corallina*). It produces gracefully arching shoots that carry pendent strings of ruby-red summer flowers against a curtain of large, heart-shaped, deep-green leaves. If you have the space, the evergreen *Magnolia grandiflora* can put on a spectacular show right at the end of the summer, when it bears huge, fragrant, snow-white, bowl-shaped flowers that emerge from furry buds.

Autumn

The perfectly named *Ceanothus* 'Autumnal Blue' is transformed late in the year when it produces fluffy clusters of intensely blue flowers. Other ceanothus varieties worth trying include 'Burkwoodii', for its bright blue flowers, and the smaller 'Perle Rose', with carmine-pink blooms.

Winter

By the onset of winter, *Garrya elliptica* 'James Roof' bears cascades of long, silvery-green catkins. Buy it in flower to be certain of getting a male plant,

which produces the most impressive catkins. Although really tough-looking, it needs some shelter – a south-, east- or west-facing wall or fence is ideal. *Clematis cirrhosa* var. *purpurascens* 'Freckles' is another reliable winter performer, producing creamy flowers speckled red. They are best seen close up, so plant it by a path or entrance.

Keeping them green

Some variegated evergreen climbers and wall shrubs are prone to sun scorch in the height of summer, especially if they run short of moisture. To help prevent water loss through evaporation, be sure to water them during periods of drought and mulch the surface of the soil.

If you'd like a pink rose to cover a wall or pergola, try 'Constance Spry'. The scented flowers are exquisite.

Fragrant and pretty, the starry pink blooms of *Jasminum × stephanense* will flower well in a sunny spot.

A warm wall will give an exotic-looking abutilon the shelter it needs to flower through the summer.

Romantic pinks

Pastel pinks are easy on the eye and generally easy to work with. They are such a diverse group of shades that it is impossible to make broad generalizations about successful associations. However, for added drama, combine pink-flowered plants with crimson or deep blue, or with white if you want to cool them down. The main clashes to avoid are yellow and pink, and orange and pink.

Pink is a very common flower colour among climbers and wall shrubs. Camellias provide some of the earliest and clearest pinks in the garden. The rose-pink peony-shaped flowers of *Camellia × williamsii* 'Debbie' look perfect against the dark green, lustrous, rounded leaves. One of the beauties of this camellia is that the fading blooms drop cleanly from the plant, so it always looks in pristine condition. The flowering quince *Chaenomeles speciosa* 'Geisha Girl' is another spring-flowering wall shrub, but

this time the blooms are a delicate shade of apricot-pink. In a mild, sheltered corner try the climbing *Jasminum × stephanense*. Blooming during early summer, it bears a succession of pretty, pale pink, highly fragrant flowers. Plant it next to a doorway, alongside a much-used path or on a patio, so its delightful perfume can be appreciated at close quarters.

Pink clematis and roses

Clematis and roses dominate the pink contribution from climbers. The vigorous *Clematis* 'Elizabeth' bears fragrant, soft-pink, late-spring and early-summer flowers. Continue the colour theme into autumn with the elegant, tulip-shaped, deep-pink flowers of *Clematis* 'Duchess of Albany' – fantastic scrambling over trellis or across the ground.

For a fence or wall in sun or dappled shade, plant the well-loved *Rosa* 'Albertine'. Its fragrant flowers are a delicate salmon-pink shade.

More pink flowers

PINK CLIMBERS
Clematis 'Apple Blossom'
Clematis 'Comtesse de Bouchaud'
Clematis 'Confetti'
Clematis 'Doctor Ruppel'
Clematis 'Markham's Pink'
Clematis 'Marjorie'
Clematis montana var. *rubens*
Clematis montana 'Tetrarose'
Clematis 'Princess Diana'
Clematis 'Willy'
Jasminum beesianum
Lathyrus latifolius 'Rosa Perle'
Lathyrus odoratus
Lonicera × americana
Rosa 'Aloha'
Rosa 'Breath of Life'
Rosa 'François Juranville'
Rosa 'Madame Grégoire Staechelin'
Rosa 'New Dawn'
Rosa 'Paul's Himalayan Musk'

PINK WALL SHRUBS
Camellia 'Inspiration'
Camellia japonica 'Elegans'
Camellia × williamsii 'Bow Bells'
Camellia × williamsii 'Dream Boat'
Chaenomeles superba 'Pink Lady'

Try pairing the white potato vine (*Solanum laxum* 'Album') with an elegant, purple-flowered clematis.

The white cup-and-saucer vine (*Cobaea scandens* f. *alba*) is perfect for an unusual, flowery screen.

For sheer sophistication, this white passion flower (*Passiflora caerulea* 'Constance Elliot') is hard to beat.

Restful whites

White, like blue, is recessive, seeming to 'sink' into the background. This is useful in a small garden, where white-flowered climbers and shrubs can be used to create the illusion of space. The flowers also seem to glow at dusk, standing out beautifully against a dark backdrop such as a hedge. Some white-flowered plants, for instance climbing hydrangeas, are useful for north-facing walls.

Clematis provide some of the best white flowers in climbing plants, especially during the spring, when the evergreen *Clematis armandii* 'Snowdrift' is smothered in deliciously scented, star-shaped, white flowers. When its flowers are over, another clematis, 'Guernsey Cream', will be in bloom, followed by the elegant 'Duchess of Edinburgh', an excellent companion for a climbing rose. When late summer arrives, the large white blooms, deep purple at the centre, of 'Alba Luxurians' will look stunning when given free rein to scramble through an established tree.

Fragrant climbers

On a sheltered wall by the patio, plant deliciously scented star jasmine (*Trachelospermum jasminoides*) or the highly fragrant common jasmine (*Jasminum officinale*). In late summer, another scented climber, the white potato vine (*Solanum laxum* 'Album') is in bloom or, if you have a large seating area, choose a white rose, such as 'Albéric Barbier' or 'Wedding Day' for masses of fragrant flowers.

Don't forget

Pale tones are useful to add light to the gloom of north-facing walls and dark corners. The cream and white splashed leaves of the variegated ivy *Hedera* 'Kolibri' will do the trick or, where you need to cover a larger surface, try the vigorous Persian ivy *Hedera colchica* 'Dentata Variegata', with its huge, heart-shaped, cream-edged, grey-green leaves. For an early summer lift in these areas you could also grow the climbing hydrangea (*Hydrangea anomala* subsp. *petiolaris*) for its large, lacy, white flowerheads.

More white flowers

WHITE CLIMBERS

Clematis 'Arctic Queen'
Clematis flammula
Clematis 'Miss Bateman'
Clematis 'White Swan'
Fallopia baldschuanica
Lathyrus latifolius 'White Pearl'
Lonicera similis var. *delavayi*
Pileostegia viburnoides
Rosa banksiae var. *banksiae*
Rosa 'Bobbie James'
Rosa 'Climbing Iceberg'
Rosa filipes 'Kiftsgate'
Rosa 'Wedding Day'
Schizophragma hydrangeoides
Trachelospermum asiaticum
Wisteria floribunda 'Alba'
Wisteria sinensis 'Alba'

WHITE WALL SHRUBS

Abeliophyllum distichum
Camellia japonica 'Nobilissima'
Carpenteria californica 'Ladham's Variety'
Chaenomeles speciosa 'Nivalis'
Chaenomeles × *superba* 'Jet Trail'
Cotoneaster horizontalis
Magnolia grandiflora

An unusual shrub for sunny walls, *Piptanthus nepalensis* is commonly known as evergreen laburnum.

Clematis tangutica is ideal if you want a climber to provide that last burst of late-summer sunshine.

Sophora microphylla 'Sun King' is a relatively new wall shrub with eye-catching, late-winter flowers.

Rich yellow and gold

Sunshine shades of yellow and gold are among the strongest colours in the spectrum, shouting out their presence in the border. All yellows appear much nearer to the eye than they are in reality, making them a useful colour to act as a distraction, or for directing the gaze. Warm and uplifting, they will tend to dominate the planting scheme around them. Yellows and golds make striking combinations with reds and oranges; acid yellows work well with greens; and pale, creamy yellows blend in with dark pinks.

Roses and climbers

The range of yellow-flowering climbers is fairly limited, with roses topping the list. The old favourite, 'Golden Showers', is a brilliant clear yellow rose, bearing its double blooms throughout the summer. Right at the beginning of the season, the charming rambler *Rosa banksiae* 'Lutea' produces garlands of small, double, violet-scented, butter-yellow blooms. In a small garden, the diminutive 'Laura Ford' is worth considering for its clusters of subtly scented, semi-double, clear yellow blooms that become tinged with pink as they age.

The late-summer *Clematis* 'Bill MacKenzie' is excellent value. Its yellow, bell-shaped flowers may be small but they are very cheering and are soon followed by charming fluffy seedheads. Winter jasmine (*Jasminum nudiflorum*) and the very fragrant honeysuckle *Lonicera japonica* 'Halliana' are also worth considering. The yellow-flowered wall shrub *Fremontodendron* needs a warm and sheltered spot.

Yellow camouflage

Yellow-variegated ivy is perfect for masking eyesores such as manhole covers and downpipes, as are variegated forms of common ivy (*Hedera helix*), for instance 'Goldchild', with yellow-edged,

More yellow flowers

YELLOW CLIMBERS
Hedera helix 'Buttercup'
Humulus lupulus 'Golden Tassels'
Jasminum humile 'Revolutum'
Jasminum officinale 'Clotted Cream'
Lonicera periclymenum 'Belgica'
Lonicera periclymenum 'Sweet Sue'
Rosa 'Gloire de Dijon'
Rosa 'The Pilgrim'
Tropaeolum peregrinum

YELLOW WALL SHRUBS
Acacia dealbata
Acacia longifolia
Coronilla valentina subsp. *glauca* 'Citrina'
Cytisus battandieri
Fremontodendron 'California Glory'

grey-green leaves, or 'Oro di Bogliasco' (formerly 'Goldheart'), with yellow-centred green leaves. For bigger cover-up jobs, try the more vigorous, larger-leaved *Hedera colchica* 'Sulphur Heart'. In sun or dappled shade, the yellow-green leaves of the golden hop (*Humulus lupulus* 'Aureus') will cover a support very quickly.

Berries and hips

If a plant produces berries, it is usually considered to be a secondary feature. For some climbers and wall shrubs, however, this is their big display time and they become festooned with showy fruit. It is true that some berry-producing plants also put on an attractive flowering performance earlier in the season, but this should be viewed as the *hors d'oeuvre* to the feast that follows.

Main-course berries

Wall shrubs can be relied on to produce the heaviest crops of berries. Perhaps the longest-lasting are the scarlet berries of the herringbone cotoneaster (*Cotoneaster horizontalis*) – loved by native songbirds and lasting well into winter. Pyracanthas also wait until autumn to reveal their bumper crops of rich-coloured fruit. *Pyracantha* 'Orange Glow', 'Dart's Red' and 'Soleil d'Or' are easy to grow and tough too, tolerating a wide range of soils and aspects and putting on a fine display even on cold, north-facing walls.

Some creepers and vines are also prolific fruit producers in autumn: Virginia creeper (*Parthenocissus quinquefolia*) and Boston ivy (*Parthenocissus tricuspidata* 'Veitchii') both produce small blue fruits. At the same time, their foliage takes on stunning autumn tints (*see* page 39).

Perfect accompaniment

A few climbing roses are grown almost as much for their end-of-season hips as for their summer flowers. One of the best is 'Madame Grégoire Staechelin'. If you have room for a rampant rambler, you might opt for 'Rambling Rector'.

Other climbers that also produce berries include oriental bittersweet (*Celastrus orbiculatus*), which bears clusters of yellow fruits in the autumn. Purple-black fruits are usually found on honeysuckles during autumn, although there are some varieties that display bright red berries after warm summers.

Pruning for more berries

Get the best display from your wall-trained pyracanthas by pruning them in the summer. On established plants that have covered their supports, prune in midsummer by carefully tipping back all new extension growth to within about 2.5cm (1in) of the base. This will encourage bushy growth of sideshoots, which should be pruned in the same way at the end of the summer. Pruning back sideshoots helps to expose the current crop of fruit for maximum impact as well as promoting better flowering – and heavier fruit crops in future. Feeding pyracanthas with a high-potash fertilizer will also help flowering and fruiting.

Don't forget

Most berry-producing climbers and wall shrubs provide birds and other garden creatures with essential winter food supplies, and are worth growing for this benefit alone (see page 22).

If you want to attract birds into your garden in winter, grow berrying shrubs.
① The golden-berried *Pyracantha* 'Soleil d'Or' and red *Pyracantha* 'Mohave'.
② The scarlet hips of *Rosa* 'Francis E. Lester'.

Purple-flowered sweet peas are some of the most desirable; be sure to choose a strongly scented one.

With its delicate, hanging flowers, *Rhodochiton atrosanguineus* is perfect for a conservatory or sheltered patio.

Clematis 'Etoile Violette' produces masses of blooms from midsummer right through to early autumn.

Serene purples

Purples can create a calming, contemplative area in the garden that is not too demanding on the eye. Used alone, purples evoke a subdued, even sombre feel and need a contrasting colour, such as silver or grey, to bring them to life. Blend purple with reds to create a brooding, mysterious atmosphere, or combine it with its opposite colour, yellow, to highlight and intensify both colours.

Velvety clematis

Oozing class and breeding, purple-flowered clematis petals seem to absorb the light and cry out to be touched. One of the darkest is 'Jackmanii Superba', with deep-violet flowers that can appear almost black in certain lights. The sumptuous blooms look most dramatic when given a contrasting backdrop, especially if allowed to scramble through a yellow-leaved host. For a complete contrast in form and habit,

try the highly fragrant *Clematis* 'Romantika'. It produces a galaxy of rich purple, star-like flowers throughout late summer – the effect is stunning when an obelisk or arch is completely covered with them.

The fast-growing Chilean potato tree *Solanum crispum* 'Glasnevin' is another purple-flowered climber that is ideal for covering the gable-end of a shed in a mild, sheltered spot. A vigorous plant, it has a veil of green stems and large, fragrant clusters of lilac-purple, starry flowers.

Purple foliage

Foliage described as purple can range from bronze through deep reds to shades of purple so dark they appear almost black in low light. The deepest purples make an excellent contrast for plants with subtle white or pink flowers or pale foliage, while the other shades are ideal for complementing closely associated colours. The best climber for purple foliage is the ornamental vine *Vitis*

vinifera 'Purpurea' (*see* opposite). Its leaves emerge pinkish white, maturing to deep red before turning purple. Grow it alongside a yellow-flowered climbing rose, such as 'Golden Showers', or the pineapple broom (*Cytisus battandieri*) for a fabulous contrast.

A few deciduous climbers and wall shrubs put on such a stunning end-of-season foliage display that they're worth growing for this alone. How long it lasts and the intensity of the colour will depend on the plants you choose as well as on seasonal variations.

Extending the display

Different plants develop their coloration at slightly different times, so you can prolong the autumn display by choosing the right combinations. The three ornamental vines – *Vitis vinifera* 'Purpurea', crimson glory vine (*Vitis coignetiae*) and Chinese Virginia creeper (*Parthenocissus henryana*) – produce their autumn colours at slightly different times, from early to late in the season. The wine-red foliage of *Vitis vinifera* 'Purpurea' turns deep purple over about a fortnight, while the crimson glory vine transforms into fiery shades of red and orange that last for four weeks or more; best of all, the Chinese Virginia creeper takes on scarlet shades for much of the autumn in a display lasting up to six weeks. Mind you, you would need quite a lot of boundary fence or a pretty big wall to grow all three together.

Disguise and transformation

Over an old tree stump or chain-link fence, let the twining stems of oriental bittersweet (*Celastrus orbiculatus*) roam free. The handsome, scalloped leaves will turn a glowing gold in early autumn and last for several weeks, just as clusters of spherical, yellow, beaded fruits appear. The white lacecap flowers of the climbing hydrangea (*Hydrangea anomala* subsp. *petiolaris*)

Red, yellow and purple tints – climbers are tremendous value in the autumn garden.
① Virginia creeper turns a brilliant red.
② *Hydrangea anomala* subsp. *petiolaris* displays luminous yellow foliage.
③ *Vitis vinifera* 'Purpurea' puts on a wonderful show of colour in autumn.

are perfect for lifting gloomy north-facing walls in summer. In autumn, this reliable climber enjoys something of a rebirth when the sombre green foliage is briefly transformed into a glowing, butter-yellow wall of light.

Variable displays

The vibrancy of autumn colour and how long it lasts vary significantly from one year to the next and from one region to another. The weather dictates, to a certain extent, the speed of leaf fall and the intensity of the display. Long, cool but frost-free nights are thought to slow down the loss of sugars from the leaves in autumn, resulting in more intense coloration. Light levels and rainfall are also thought to be contributing factors. If the weather is calm during this period, the leaves will remain in place for longer, extending the display.

Plants for a purpose

Use these lists to help you to choose the right climbers and wall shrubs for a range of specific purposes, conditions or effects. *See also* A–Z directory, pages 73–105.

The crimson glory vine (*Vitis coignetiae*) has fabulous autumn colour that lasts for a month or more. It is ideal for a substantial pergola or against a wall.

Best for doorways and small arches

CLIMBERS

Clematis cirrhosa var. *purpurascens* 'Freckles'
Clematis 'Jackmanii Superba'
Clematis 'Polish Spirit'
Clematis 'Royal Velours'
Jasminum officinale 'Fiona Sunrise'
Lonicera periclymenum 'Serotina'
Lonicera similis var. *delavayi*
Rosa 'New Dawn'
Rosa 'A Shropshire Lad'
Solanum laxum 'Album'
Trachelospermum jasminoides

Best for pillars, posts and obelisks

CLIMBERS

Clematis 'Prince Charles'
Clematis 'Wisley'
Eccremocarpus scaber
Hedera helix 'Goldchild'
Humulus lupulus 'Aureus'
Ipomoea purpurea 'Heavenly Blue'
Lathyrus odoratus 'Cupani'
Lonicera periclymenum 'Sweet Sue'
Rosa 'Aloha'
Rosa 'The Pilgrim'
Rosa 'Warm Welcome'
Thunbergia alata

Best for large, sturdy pergolas

CLIMBERS

Actinidia deliciosa
Akebia quinata
Campsis × *tagliabuana* 'Madame Galen'
Clematis 'Bill MacKenzie'
Clematis 'Elizabeth'
Lonicera × *americana*
Rosa 'Paul's Himalayan Musk'
Vitis coignetiae
Vitis vinifera 'Schiava Grossa'
Wisteria floribunda
Wisteria sinensis

Best for containers

CLIMBERS

Actinidia pilosula
Clematis 'Evening Star'
Clematis 'Kingfisher'
Euonymus fortunei 'Silver Queen'
Ipomoea lobata
Passiflora 'Eden'
Rhodochiton atrosanguineus
Thunbergia alata
Trachelospermum jasminoides 'Variegatum'

WALL SHRUBS

Abutilon 'Kentish Belle'
Camellia × *williamsii* 'Anticipation'
Chaenomeles speciosa 'Geisha Girl'
Sophora microphylla 'Sun King'

Best for warm, sunny walls

CLIMBERS

Actinidia kolomikta
Campsis grandiflora
Clematis armandii
Cobaea scandens
Jasminum officinale f. *affine*
Passiflora caerulea
Rosa 'Etoile de Hollande'

WALL SHRUBS

Abeliophyllum distichum
Abutilon megapotamicum
Acacia dealbata
Callistemon citrinus 'Splendens'
Ceanothus 'Concha'
Coronilla valentina subsp. *glauca* 'Citrina'
Cytisus battandieri
Fremontodendron californicum

Best for cold, sunless walls

CLIMBERS

Akebia quinata
Euonymus fortunei 'Emerald Gaiety'
Hedera colchica 'Dentata Variegata'
Hedera helix 'Oro di Bogliasco' ('Goldheart')
Hydrangea anomala subsp. *petiolaris*
Jasminum nudiflorum
Parthenocissus tricuspidata 'Veitchii'

WALL SHRUBS

Camellia japonica 'Elegans'
Chaenomeles speciosa 'Moerloosei'
Cotoneaster horizontalis
Garrya elliptica
Pyracantha 'Mohave'

Fastest-growing

Campsis radicans
Clematis montana var. *rubens*
Clematis 'Purpurea Plena Elegans'
Fallopia baldschuanica
Humulus lupulus 'Aureus'
Lathyrus latifolius 'White Pearl'
Lonicera japonica 'Halliana'
Parthenocissus quinquefolia
Passiflora caerulea

Best for ground cover

CLIMBERS

Clematis 'Alba Luxurians'
Clematis 'Frances Rivis'
Clematis 'Madame Julia Correvon'
Hedera colchica 'Sulphur Heart'
Hedera helix 'Glacier'
Lonicera japonica var. *repens*

WALL SHRUBS

Ceanothus thyrsiflorus var. *repens*
Cotoneaster horizontalis
Euonymus fortunei 'Emerald 'n' Gold'

Best for fragrance

CLIMBERS

Clematis 'Elizabeth'
Clematis × *triternata* 'Rubromarginata'
Jasminum officinale f. *affine*
Jasminum polyanthum
Lonicera japonica 'Halliana'
Lonicera periclymenum 'Graham Thomas'
Rosa banksiae var. *banksiae*
Rosa filipes 'Kiftsgate'
Rosa 'Rambling Rector'
Trachelospermum asiaticum

WALL SHRUBS

Abeliophyllum distichum
Acacia dealbata
Cytisus battandieri
Magnolia grandiflora

Most indestructible

CLIMBERS

Clematis 'Frances Rivis'
Clematis montana 'Tetrarose'
Clematis viticella 'Mary Rose'
Fallopia baldschuanica
Hedera colchica 'Sulphur Heart'
Humulus lupulus 'Aureus'
Jasminum nudiflorum
Parthenocissus tricuspidata 'Veitchii'
Solanum laxum 'Album'

WALL SHRUBS

Cotoneaster horizontalis
Euonymus fortunei 'Emerald Gaiety'

Best for autumn flowers and foliage

CLIMBERS

Ampelopsis megalophylla
Vitis 'Brant'
Vitis coignetiae

WALL SHRUBS

Ceanothus 'Autumnal Blue'
Cotoneaster atropurpureus 'Variegatus'
Cotoneaster horizontalis
Parthenocissus henryana

Best for berries, fruits and seedheads

CLIMBERS

Actinidia deliciosa
Billardiera longiflora
Celastrus orbiculatus
Clematis 'Bill MacKenzie'
Clematis tangutica
Clematis tibetana subsp. *vernayi*
Rosa 'Madame Grégoire Staechelin'
Rosa 'Rambling Rector'
Vitis vinifera 'Schiava Grossa'

WALL SHRUBS

Chaenomeles speciosa 'Nivalis'
Cotoneaster horizontalis
Piptanthus nepalensis
Pyracantha
Wisteria formosa

Best to attract wildlife

CLIMBERS

Celastrus orbiculatus
Clematis tangutica
Hedera helix
Humulus lupulus 'Aureus'
Hydrangea anomala subsp. *petiolaris*
Lonicera periclymenum 'Belgica'
Rosa filipes 'Kiftsgate'
Vitis 'Brant'

WALL SHRUBS

Ceanothus 'Puget Blue'
Cotoneaster horizontalis
Pyracantha coccinea 'Red Column'

Most long-flowering

CLIMBERS

Clematis 'Lady Northcliffe'
Clematis 'Purpurea Plena Elegans'
Eccremocarpus scaber
Lathyrus latifolius 'White Pearl'
Passiflora 'White Lightning'
Rhodochiton atrosanguineus
Rosa 'Madame Alfred Carrière'
Rosa 'Teasing Georgia'
Solanum laxum 'Album'

WALL SHRUBS

Abutilon megapotamicum 'Variegatum'
Ceanothus × *delileanus* 'Gloire de Versailles'
Fremontodendron 'California Glory'

Best evergreens

CLIMBERS

Billardiera longifolia
Clematis armandii 'Enham Star'
Clematis cirrhosa var. *balearica*
Dregea sinensis
Hedera colchica 'Sulphur Heart'
Hedera helix 'Goldchild'
Holboellia coriacea
Passiflora caerulea
Trachelospermum jasminoides

WALL SHRUBS

Camellia japonica 'Adolphe Audusson'
Ceanothus 'Concha'
Magnolia grandiflora
Pyracantha 'Saphyr Orange'

Best for winter flowers

CLIMBERS

Clematis cirrhosa var. *balearica*
Clematis napaulensis
Jasminum nudiflorum

WALL SHRUBS

Abeliophyllum distichum
Acacia dealbata 'Gaulois Astier'
Camellia sasanqua 'Crimson King'
Coronilla valentina subsp. *glauca*
Garrya elliptica

Planting and growing

Most climbers and wall shrubs are very easy to grow provided you choose the right plant for the situation. Keep them happy by watering and feeding when necessary, and keep tying in new growth so they don't run riot. For the best flowering performance, however, familiarize yourself with a few of the pruning basics so that you know exactly how and when to cut them back. Then jot down a note in your gardening diary so you don't forget.

Tools and equipment

If you have a lot of wall shrubs and climbers in your garden, you will need – in addition to the standard range of cultivation tools – special tools for pruning. Most climbers and wall shrubs can be pruned successfully using a pair of secateurs, but for mature plants you might need loppers and a good-quality pruning saw. You will also need to provide some method of support and training, which will include wires and trellis.

Whichever type of secateurs you use for pruning, make sure you keep the blades sharp and clean.

Pruning tools

Secateurs are fine for most types of light pruning. There are two basic types, with different cutting actions. 'Bypass' have a scissor-like action, while 'anvil' secateurs have a single blade that cuts against a metal block and a guillotine-like action. However, if stems are over 1cm (½in) thick, or you find pruning difficult, a pair of long-handled loppers will make life easier and do a better job, too. For really old, woody stems more than 2.5cm (1in) thick, you would be wise to invest in a pointed pruning saw. The teeth will make short work of even the toughest stems.

Supports and fixings

Climbers on walls and fences need the support of strong wires fixed to the surface with vine-eyes (see pages 50–2). Use tensioning bolts to keep the wires tight. And, if you want to grow a climber or wall shrub on a brick wall, a drill with a masonry bit is an essential piece of kit. Ready-made wooden trellis is fine for plants that are fairly light; or you can make your own using sturdy, pressure-treated timber.

Freestanding support can be in the form of obelisks, arches and pergolas – all available ready-made or in kit form. Obelisks are generally wrought iron or woven wickerwork. Arches and pergolas are often timber but you can get attractive, if a bit more expensive, plastic-coated metal structures. The key is to buy sturdy, well-made structures that will take the weight of a full-grown climber, and install them securely.

Don't forget

For tall climbers above head height, you might like to buy a pole pruner, which has a secateur head and sometimes a pruning saw at the end of a long handle.

Keep a few bits and bobs to hand so that you can carry out running repairs to supports and tie in wayward shoots whenever you're out in the garden.

Growing conditions

Although soils vary widely from garden to garden and place to place, all soils are made up of the same basic ingredients: clay, silt and sand, plus organic matter. It is the proportions of these ingredients in your particular garden soil that largely determine its fertility and how easy it is to work.

Soil types

Climbers and wall shrubs are permanent plants that depend on the soil for moisture and nutrients. The soil next to walls can be impoverished and dry, making life more difficult for the plants growing there. In new gardens, the soil in borders close to buildings is often a poor-quality mix of subsoil strewn with builders' rubble and debris, and this will need to be substantially improved or even replaced. Before you can start making improvements to your soil, you need to understand a little more about it.

In heavy ground there is a high proportion of clay particles, which

pack together very tightly leaving few air spaces. This is why clay soils do not drain freely. Although often very fertile, clay soils are difficult to work, because they remain wet for longer after rainfall, making the particles stick to your tools and boots. Clay soils are also easily

Well-rotted manure is without doubt the best food for your soil, adding nutrients and improving texture. If you want to give your plants a head start, use plenty of it.

compacted when walked on, further reducing drainage and inhibiting root growth.

Sandy soil is very light, dry to the touch and gritty. Pick up a handful and it will flow through your fingers.

Chalky soil is easy to identify owing to the very visible lumps of chalk. It tends to dry out fairly rapidly.

Clay soil is sticky, fertile and usually moist to the touch. When really dry, it bakes hard and cracks.

Light soils generally contain a higher proportion of sandy particles. These are large and irregular in shape, so don't pack together very tightly, leaving lots of air pockets. This allows water to drain freely, but, unfortunately, the water-soluble nutrients in sandy soils are easily washed out (a process known as leaching), impoverishing the soil. The good news is that sandy soils are easy to work, even in winter, and because they warm up

quickly are ideal for making early sowings outdoors, perhaps of hardy annual sweet peas in spring.

Silt particles fall between sand and clay in size and shape. Soils that contain a lot of silt are usually fertile and drain reasonably freely, but do not dry out quickly. Like clay soils, they are easily compacted.

Most normal soils contain a proportion of each of these ingredients: they drain reasonably well, are fairly fertile and do not dry out too quickly – ideal conditions for plant growth.

The acid test

Before making plant selections, it is also essential that you know the pH level of your soil – that is how acid or alkaline it is – because this may limit the types of plants you can grow. The pH level is measured on a scale of 1 (very acid) to 14 (very alkaline), with 7 being neutral.

Several wall shrubs, including camellia, *Acacia*, *Berberidopsis*, *Desfontainia*, pineapple broom (*Cytisus*) and magnolia, prefer a slightly acid soil, while ivies, vines and *Fremontodendron* like a slightly

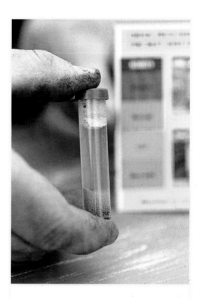

Before deciding which plants to buy, it's a good idea to check the level of your soil's acidity. Simple soil-test kits are available in most garden centres.

alkaline soil. Fortunately, most plants aren't too fussy and will grow happily in soil that is slightly alkaline to slightly acidic.

Improving your soil

No matter what type of soil you have, it can be improved using organic matter, such as well-rotted farmyard manure or garden compost. This lovely stuff is the cure-all solution to most soil ills: it improves the soil structure and drainage of heavy soils, and it increases the water-holding capacity and available nutrients in light soils. The traditional way to incorporate organic matter into your soil was to dig it in. But more recent research suggests that for most soils the best option is to spread it on the surface and let the soil organisms do the work for you.

Loam is wonderful stuff. Rich and brown, it holds together when moist without being sticky.

Peat is very dark in colour and although low in nutrients it holds large amounts of water.

Choosing and buying climbers

Most garden centres have a specialist area dedicated to climbers. If you buy late in the season, climbers can become overgrown and even tangled together or, if not properly supported, blown over and damaged by wind and rain. Go shopping during the spring, once new stock has arrived, and you will find the best quality and the widest choice.

Selecting the right plant

When selecting a new climber look for one with several strong stems growing up from the base and fresh, healthy-looking leaves with no signs of pests or diseases. Once you're happy with your choice, make sure the position and the support you have in mind for your climber are big enough, otherwise you may end up having to cut it back annually and miss out on much of the flowering potential. Similarly, if you want to cover a large expanse of wall or trellis, then make sure the

There is a bewildering number of clematis varieties. For help with your choices visit a specialist nursery.

plant you buy will be vigorous enough for the job. Matching vigour to site is particularly important for climbers being trained into an established tree or hedge.

Although most climbers and wall shrubs aren't too fussy when it comes to soil type, there are exceptions, so always check before you start. Climbers and wall shrubs also vary in their need for sunlight and shelter. Sun-loving climbers planted in dappled shade may grow and flower disappointingly and in deep shade will probably fail to get established, while shade-tolerant plants in full sun are liable to be scorched and may die.

Young climbing plants will need some form of support for their growing stems, such as wooden sticks, while still in their pots.

Maintenance

It makes sense to match the climber you want to the amount of time you can spend looking after it. High-maintenance climbers, such as roses, require annual pruning and training and will perform well only if you are able to meet their needs. However, there are many easy-care climbers on offer that look just as good. If you're planting two climbers together, it's also a smart move to choose plants with similar pruning requirements to help cut down on maintenance time.

Don't forget

Most climbers are reasonably fast-growing, so there's little benefit in buying a more expensive, larger plant. The exception to this perhaps is wisteria, when it's worth paying extra for a grafted plant.

Planting climbers and wall shrubs

Hardy climbers and wall shrubs that have been raised in containers can be planted at any time, provided the soil is not frozen or waterlogged. On well-drained soils, planting in autumn is a good idea because the plants will then be able to get established before the summer. If you garden on heavy clay, however, it will be easier to plant in spring, once the soil becomes workable. Evergreen climbers and wall shrubs are best planted in spring – on all soil types – so they have time to get established before the cold winter weather sets in.

Off to a good start

Before planting, thoroughly water climbers and wall shrubs in their pots. Then add a slow-release fertilizer to the planting hole, as well as plenty of well-rotted organic manure or compost. Climbers to be trained up walls and fences will need to be planted away from the support and set at an angle back from it so that the rootball can expand into fresh soil on all sides and establish itself quickly. Set the crown of most climbers at the same depth as it is in the pot, once the soil has been firmed with your heel. The exception to this rule is clematis (*see* page 48). After watering thoroughly, apply a thick mulch around each plant but don't pile it up against the stems.

When you are planting wall shrubs, dig a hole about twice as wide and deep as the rootball, mix some organic matter into the bottom of the hole and then create a slight mound to stand the rootball on. Make sure that the top of the rootball is at the same height as the

When planting against freestanding supports without foundations you can dig a hole right alongside and train the plant up vertically.

surrounding soil. Backfill with soil and firm with your heel to remove any air pockets. After watering thoroughly, apply a thick mulch.

Deep-planting clematis

Clematis are, unfortunately, prone to a fungal disease known as clematis wilt (*see* page 71). Guard against this disease by planting them 10–15cm (4–6in) deeper than in their original pot so that the base of each stem is covered with about 8cm (3in) of soil. If the disease strikes and infects the leaves above ground, the dormant buds below the soil surface might well survive and reshoot.

Give a newly purchased clematis a thorough soaking in a bucket of water before you plant it out.

Insert a cut-down plastic bottle next to the plant and water into it so the moisture goes directly to the roots.

HOW TO plant a clematis against a wall

House walls can be very dry at the base. Brickwork absorbs moisture from the soil and the eaves can stop rainwater reaching the ground directly beneath them.

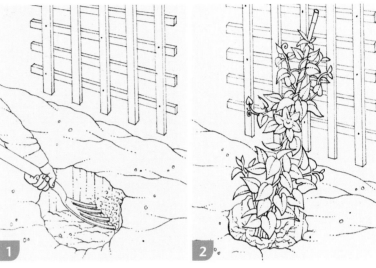

1 Dig a hole at least 30cm (12in) away from the base of the wall and make sure it is wide and deep enough to accommodate the rootball of the clematis comfortably. Add some slow-release fertilizer.

2 Plant the clematis at about 10–15cm (4–6in) deeper than it was in the original pot at an angle of 45°. Leave the canes in place, leaning them towards the wall so they protect the vulnerable young stems.

3 After backfilling with soil and gently firming to get rid of any air pockets, water the clematis thoroughly to make sure the soil settles around the roots. Add a layer of mulch to help retain moisture.

4 Add more supporting canes and tease out the stems, cutting any plastic ties still in place. Tie the stems loosely to the canes with soft garden twine and, finally, secure the canes to the trellis.

Planting in containers

Nearly all climbers and wall shrubs can be grown in containers, and growing them this way also offers several advantages. Firstly, it allows you to grow climbers and wall shrubs that might struggle to survive elsewhere in your garden and, secondly, if you have chalky soil you can grow acid-loving plants in pots filled with ericaceous compost.

Growing plants in containers also allows you to try slightly more exotic plants. Frost-tender plants can be placed on the patio during the summer months to enjoy the best of the weather and can then be moved under cover to a frost-free area for the winter months.

Add a thick mulch of pebbles to containers in a sunny spot to keep clematis roots cool and moist.

Repotting

If a climber or wall shrub is relatively new and easy to lift, it will need repotting each spring into a larger-sized pot until it is in its final container, which is usually at least 45cm (18in) deep and wide. Each time you repot, use a loam-based compost (or, for acid-loving plants, ericaceous compost). You can add water-retaining gel to increase the period between waterings, as well as a balanced slow-release fertilizer each spring so you don't have to feed during the growing season. Once the plant is too big to repot, just skim off the top few centimetres of old compost each spring and replace it with fresh. A slow-release fertilizer can be added at this time, too.

HOW TO | plant a climber in a container

Climbers are adaptable and well suited to growing in containers. When planting them the most important thing is to make sure the pot is deep and wide enough to accommodate the plant's roots comfortably, allowing them to spread and grow.

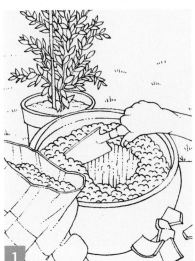

1 Place pieces of broken flowerpot into the base of the pot for drainage, then add loam-based compost. Sink the potted climber into the compost to make a hole that is just the right size for the rootball.

2 After watering well and removing the climber from its pot, gently lower it into the hole you created in the fresh compost. Leave a 3–4cm (1½in) gap between the compost and rim to allow for watering.

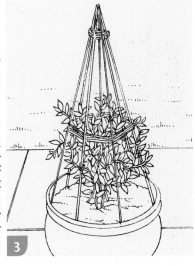

3 Now your climber is settled happily in its pot, all it needs is a support to grow up. A wicker or willow wigwam is ideal and can be inserted into the pot just after planting. Make sure the support is firmly in place.

Supporting on walls and fences

Most climbers and all wall shrubs will need some sort of support if they are to cover a wall neatly and evenly. For large expanses of wall, the best way of providing support is to use fencing wire. Trellis is a good option for smaller areas. Whatever method of support you employ, it's important that you carry out regular maintenance checks.

Wire supports

To cover a large area of fence or wall, use strong, galvanized fencing wire, equally spaced over the surface. Keep wires horizontal for most climbers and wall shrubs, but a vertical or fan-shaped arrangement works best for twining climbers. If you're feeling adventurous, you can attach the wires in other shapes or formations, for example making an arch around a door. The wires will be practically invisible to the naked eye and they will be a lot cheaper than trellis for covering large areas.

For most climbers 10-gauge galvanized wire will suffice, but for very vigorous or heavy climbers opt for the stronger 14-gauge instead, held taut by a straining bolt at one end. Space the wires in parallel formation (unless you're creating a fan shape) about 45cm (18in) apart, so that they're held about 5–8cm (2–3in) from the wall using vine-eyes, which are specifically designed for the purpose. This gap is to allow for air circulation and to prevent the wall from becoming damp and fungal diseases attacking the climber.

Strong, horizontal wires held securely by vine-eyes will be virtually invisible to the naked eye when covered by a mature climbing rose.

Don't forget

Even self-clinging climbers, such as ivies and vines, will need a little help to get started. Simply damping the wall down from time to time will make it easier for the climbers to get a firm grip.

Maintaining walls and fences

All supports will need maintenance every so often. Many climbers and wall shrubs are long-lived, so you may have to replace the supports altogether when they reach the end of their useful life. Wires stretch and rust where the galvanized covering has worn away, while untreated trellis can rot or simply fall apart with age. The wall or fence that provides the support may also need routine maintenance.

There are two main types of vine-eyes: the first looks like a triangular nail and is hammered into the mortar between courses of bricks or blocks; the second type is a threaded eyelet. Eyelets are screwed into holes drilled with a masonry bit and filled with wall plugs. If the mortar is very hard, you can make guide holes using a fine masonry bit before hammering in the triangular vine-eyes, too. The screw-in eyelets can also be used to attach wires to fences and other wooden structures.

Trellis

Ready-made trellis is available in panels or fancy shapes that can look decorative in their own right. The most important thing is to buy a strong trellis that is up to the job of supporting your climber for many years. For unusual shapes or awkward corners you could buy wooden battens that have been pressure-treated with a preservative and make your own trellis. With all types of trellis, use spacer blocks or battens to hold it about 4cm (1½in) away from the wall. Strong trellis can be used either to make free-standing screens for attaching to fencing posts or for extending the height of existing fences. Plastic-

Sturdy trellis clothed in leafy climbers can be used as a see-through garden divider. It will also help to screen out unwanted buildings without blocking too much light.

coated wire mesh or even galvanized mesh also makes a good support for climbers and wall shrubs. Although less aesthetically pleasing than a wooden trellis, coated or galvanized mesh is extremely versatile and can be bent to make curves – perhaps to cover a downpipe. And as part of a contemporary garden design galvanized trellis can in fact look very striking.

Attaching the plants

Train climbers towards the wall or fence using canes to spread out the stems. On a wall in an exposed site, hold the stems against the surface

Ensure trellis is securely screwed onto spacing battens fixed to the wall or fence so air can circulate behind the climber.

using plant ties fixed to the wall or to nails hammered in at strategic points.

When tying in the plants to their support, make sure the stems remain in front, to keep the air space behind as clear as possible. This will also make pruning straightforward and essential maintenance easier at those times when you might need to lower the climber from the wall or trellis.

Checking trellis

If you have sufficient space, climbers with flexible stems can be untied from their supports after pruning and carefully lowered to the ground. Bear in mind you will need as much room on the floor as the climber covers on the vertical structure. If the trellis is in good shape and you simply need to access the wall for repairs, it may be easier to unscrew the trellis from its spacing battens and carefully lower it to the floor, with the climber still attached. For walls that will need regular maintenance, such as repainting, you might be better off planning ahead and creating a hinged trellis that can simply be lowered from the wall like the back door of a horse box, to give you the necessary access.

Checking wires

Wires will also need to be untied and lowered to the ground to allow for routine maintenance. Replace any stretched or corroded wires and tension all those that are in good condition by adjusting the straining bolt at the end of each wire. Also check that none of the vine-eyes have become loose; if they have, reposition or cement them back in. Take this opportunity to check the wall and make any necessary repairs.

Maintaining fences

Wooden fences, like trellis, tend to fall apart with age. Well-constructed, pressure-treated fences may last ten years or even longer if they're maintained regularly. Replace post caps and the top rail of panel fences by cannibalizing one sound existing panel to repair all the others. This keeps costs down and gives the fence a uniform look.

HOW TO put up wall wires

A series of heavy-gauge wires spaced about 45cm (18in) apart on a brick wall and held taut with vine-eyes makes an ideal support for climbing roses and wall shrubs with stiff stems. It is fairly quick and simple to put up if you have a drill with a masonry bit.

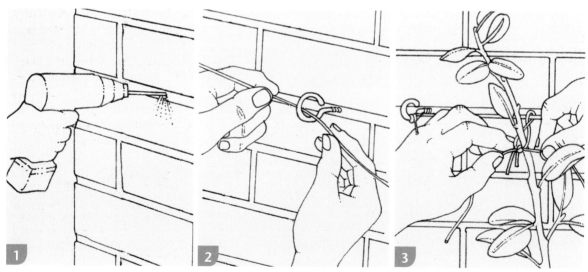

1 Put a mark on the wall in the mortar between the bricks indicating where you want to fix the wires. Drill holes into the mortar for the vine-eyes, making them slightly longer than the threads.

2 After firmly pushing a wall plug into each hole, screw in the vine-eye so that the wire can be threaded straight through it. Bend the wire round the 'eye' at the end of the wall to secure it.

3 Using soft twine in a natural colour, tie the stems of the climber to the wire at regular intervals. Match the strength of the twine to the vigour of the climber and tie in new growth when it appears.

Watering and feeding

Climbers and wall shrubs are frequently grown in situations where the soil is dry and impoverished. If you have limited time to water and feed the plants in your garden, concentrate your efforts on plants grown in containers, new plants, plants in borders next to walls, and plants in dry spots under trees and next to hedges, especially near evergreens.

Watering wisely

On light, free-draining soils watering is more critical and shortages become more acute, more quickly. However, once garden plants are well established most won't need much watering at all, except in prolonged hot, dry periods. On the other hand, young plants, those that have recently been planted and, above all, plants in patio containers, need regular moisture. The best times to water are in the early morning or in the evening, as water will evaporate more slowly at these times of day.

Watering might seem simple, but it's often where beginner gardeners, as well as some experienced ones, come unstuck. The key to success is to water where and when it's needed. Do not be tempted to water little and often, as this will increase water loss through evaporation (only the surface layer of the soil or compost gets wet). It also encourages surface rooting, which makes plants susceptible to drought. Ideally, you should water thoroughly and leave longer periods between watering: ensure that you soak the whole rootball each time you water and don't water again until the plant needs it – that is, when the soil is dry to the touch. For dry borders next to walls or hedges, consider a leaky hose, buried out of sight.

Don't forget

If you live in a hard-water area, the easiest method for watering acid-loving climbers, such as *Berberidopsis* and *Billardiera,* or wall shrubs like the pineapple broom (*Cytisus battandieri*) and camellia, is collecting slightly acidic rainwater from a convenient downpipe.

Water butts need not be ugly. Old, well-coopered beer barrels are very attractive and surprisingly durable.

Feeding

Most climbers and wall shrubs don't require much routine feeding once established, unless they're on poor soil next to a house wall or by an established tree. If this is the case, apply a balanced general fertilizer during late winter or early spring and always follow the instructions on the packet – adding more than the recommended amount is not necessarily beneficial.

Good nutrition

Most general-purpose fertilizers provide a balanced combination of the nutrients that plants need for

Spent mushroom compost has a fairly good balance of nutrients, but avoid it if you want your garden to be peat-free.

healthy growth. Put simply, the major nutrients plants require are: nitrogen (N) for shoot and leaf growth; phosphorus (P) for root growth; and potash or potassium (K) for flowers and fruit. Other minerals and trace elements are also beneficial for plant growth and these will often be added to better-quality proprietary fertilizers. If you garden organically, use an approved fertilizer such as blood, fish and bone instead. And if you would prefer to avoid animal-based

products, there are several preparations based on seaweed.

Some free-flowering climbers, such as roses and clematis, will put on improved displays if you pamper them with a high-potash feed during spring and again in early summer. High-potash preparations include tomato food, which you can buy in liquid form and dilute before applying. Organic high-potash feeds are also available.

Acid-loving wall shrubs such as camellias, however, need fertilizers that have a high proportion of iron to keep their foliage green and healthy. Look for 'ericaceous' or 'acid-loving' preparations, especially if you have mature shrubs that would benefit from a tonic.

Don't forget

Most varieties of potting compost contain enough plant nutrients to feed a climber or wall shrub only for the first six weeks after it has been planted. After this time the nutrients will have been exhausted, so apply a liquid feed fortnightly during the growing season to keep it growing and flowering well.

If a slow-release fertilizer hasn't been added to the potting compost, a liquid feed will give a boost to permanent climbers and wall shrubs in containers.

Weed control

Weeds are just as likely to gain a foothold in soil next to structures supporting climbers and wall shrubs as elsewhere in the garden. Climbing weeds, such as bindweed, can be a particular nuisance, especially if you have climbers growing up obelisks and posts in the middle of a border. Keep an eye out for weeds in inaccessible areas next to walls and fences, and take steps to control them before they get established.

Bindweed sends out deep, brittle roots that are devilishly difficult to remove and will resprout at the drop of a hat.

Weeds fall into two camps: annual, such as groundsel and chickweed, and perennial, like dock and thistle. Annual weeds germinate, grow, flower and set seed in the same year and then die. Perennials live longer and set seed year after year, although some, like bindweed, also colonize the ground by underground roots that spread unseen. You can prevent weeds from gaining the upper hand in your garden by covering bare patches, employing mulches, and using climbers and other ground-cover plants to smother them.

Annual weeds are easy to control by hand-weeding, where practical, or routine hoeing. However, do take care not to damage the stems of fleshy climbers while you're using a hoe. Perennial weeds, on the other hand, must be removed with their roots intact, otherwise they'll just regrow.

Mulching

Mulching is a good way to keep the base of climbers and wall shrubs moist and weed-free. A mulch is simply a loose layer of material placed on the surface of the soil. Organic mulches include well-rotted garden compost or leaf mould, while gravel and pebbles, weed-suppressing fabrics and black polythene are all inorganic. Mulching has many benefits in addition to suppressing weeds and reducing moisture loss from the soil through evaporation. Mulches also act as insulators, keeping the soil warm in the winter and cool in the summer.

Don't forget

If you have to use weedkillers, make sure that you protect nearby climbers and wall shrubs with plastic sheeting and don't remove the covering until the spray is dry.

Established clumps of bramble should be cut back hard. Any regrowth can be torched using a flame gun.

Nettles are easy to pull up as long as you cover up arms and hands. Any remaining yellow roots won't regrow.

Keep on top of annual chickweed by removing it at the seedling stage before it can form dense mats.

Pruning and training

If left to their own devices, climbers and wall shrubs would soon outgrow their allotted space and lose their ornamental appeal. Most climbers would also produce all their new growth and flowers out of sight at the top of the plant, leaving the base to become woody and bare. Pruning and training encourages them to produce more flowers and fruit and keeps them healthy by letting in light and air.

Routine pruning

Some climbers and wall shrubs respond to routine pruning once or twice a year, while others can be left for several seasons before you have to get the secateurs out. How and when you prune a particular plant will depend on what you are trying to achieve and how the plant grows. The most important thing is not to prune out all the growth that will produce the plant's main feature – usually the next crop of flowers or berries. The more vigorous self-clinging climbers, such as creepers and vines, will require regular pruning to prevent them interfering with windows, guttering and any overhead cables. Wayward shoots produced away

Persuade climbing roses to produce more flowers along their sideshoots by bending their long, trailing stems into a horizontal position.

from the support will also need tying in or cutting out.

Wall shrubs are more easy-going and may well need just a general trim to keep them in shape. All wall shrubs need tying into their support at least once a year to help direct the growth, to get even cover and to prevent the plant leaning away from the vertical surface.

Training young climbers

A young and healthy climber with several vigorous stems is fairly easy to get established on its support. Release the stems carefully from the canes that were supporting them in the pot and tie each shoot into the bottom of the support, so that they are well spaced out. If you're

---

Where to make a pruning cut

Cut diagonally just above the bud (below left) when pruning climbers and wall shrubs with buds arranged alternately on the stem, such as wisteria. The cut should slope down behind the bud – ideally at an angle of about 25 degrees – to prevent moisture running into the bud. For climbers and wall shrubs with opposite buds, make a horizontal cut straight across the stem, about 6mm (¼in) above a pair of buds.

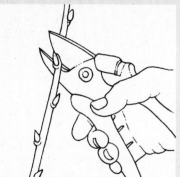

Angled cut above an alternate bud

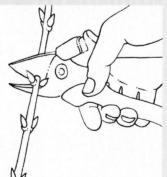

Straight cut above a pair of buds

Don't forget

Climbers with variegated leaves can, from time to time, produce all-green shoots. These need to be pruned out. They are more vigorous than the variegated leaves and, if left, will swamp them, turning the whole climber green.

planting against a garden structure that doesn't have foundations, such as a post or an obelisk, the climber can be set right next to its support and trained directly up it. Most climbers will need tying into the support to keep them secure and to direct the growth where it is wanted. Even self-clinging climbers will require some guidance to achieve even coverage.

Training young wall shrubs

Wall shrubs with woody stems, including cotoneaster and pyracantha, can be trained against a vertical surface using a trellis. They will need tying in regularly to encourage them not to grow outwards, which is their natural habit. With a flexi-stemmed shrub, such as winter jasmine, you can achieve a simple fan shape straight after planting if the plant has good, strong stems. Simply space these out and tie them into the support.

Pruning established climbers

Climbers in permanent positions need routine pruning to keep them flowering well and in good health. Remove dead, dying, diseased and damaged stems as soon as you spot them, as well as any weak or spindly shoots. Make sure you dispose of any diseased material and clean your pruning tools after each cut, to help prevent disease spreading.

Pruning established wall shrubs

Some routine pruning is necessary to keep wall shrubs looking good. Camellias just need a short back and sides to cut back most of the previous year's growth, while *Garrya elliptica* should have only wayward or overlong shoots cut back. A few flowering wall shrubs, including evergreen ceanothus, will need one third of the previous season's growth removed, and mature, thicket-forming shrubs, such as winter jasmine, should have one in three of the oldest stems removed each year. On shrubs that produce flowers on spurs, like flowering quince (*Chaenomeles*), new growth can be cut back to within a few leaves of the old.

HOW TO prune and train a young climber

To create a really strong framework, start training young climbers soon after planting. For the first few years a new climber should need little pruning, but make sure you train and tie in the stems regularly.

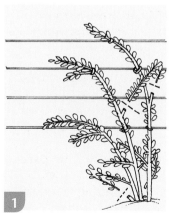

1 Immediately after planting select the most vigorous stems, then position and tie them into the support. Prune out any damaged stems and remove any stems you don't need as part of the framework. This will promote strong new growth. Throughout the growing season, keep training new growth and tying it into position.

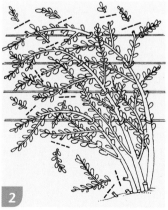

2 Cut back all sideshoots close to the main stem in spring and remove any growth that has been damaged by frost. Consider the shape of the climber and cut out overcrowded growth and any stems that spoil it. Space out the remaining shoots on the support, tying them into position to form a strong framework.

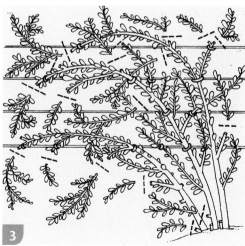

3 Cut back each of the strongest stems by up to one third in subsequent years. This will encourage new shoots to form and extend the framework of the plant. Remove any unwanted stems and cut back weak or spindly shoots to two buds. Tie in all the main stems and continue to train and guide them as they grow.

Pruning roses

Most roses require little or no formative pruning, although you can tip-prune climbing roses during the first spring after planting to encourage dormant buds to shoot. Ramblers, on the other hand, should be pruned straight after planting. Cut all stems back to about 45cm (18in) from ground level to encourage new shoots to sprout from the base.

Pruning for more flowers

When it comes to pruning to encourage more prolific flowering, climbing and rambling roses can be divided into the following main groups:

Climbing roses Most climbing roses are repeat-flowering, blooming throughout the summer. As with modern bush roses, prune in late autumn or winter, after flowering has finished. Cut back the flowering sideshoots to a couple of buds.

For well-established climbing roses that produce a single flush of flowers, remove up to one third of the oldest stems after flowering, cutting them back to a young sideshoot near the base.

Rambling roses Prune rambling roses directly after flowering. Cut

Dead-heading roses during the growing season will encourage them to produce more blooms and keep the show going.

Remember to protect the long stems of climbing and rambling roses from wind damage by tying them into the support.

back the old stems that have finished flowering to a young sideshoot lower down. If there are new vigorous shoots sprouting from the base, cut out one old, exhausted stem for each new shoot.

Ground-cover roses Low-growing shrub roses, such as those in the Flower Carpet group, need little pruning. To keep them bushy, tip-prune extension growth and remove any stems that are growing vertically.

HOW TO prune and train a mature climbing rose

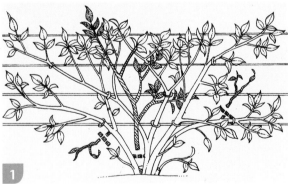

1 In the autumn, remove any dead, damaged, dying or diseased stems from the plant. Also prune out any thin, weak, spindly growth, and let in light and air by removing congested shoots from the centre of the climber. When the new season's stems appear, train and tie them into the wires.

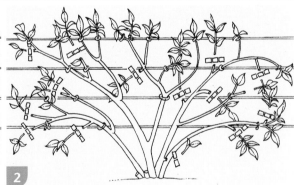

2 Remove crossing stems and train the remaining stems sideways along the wires, bending them down gently so they are horizontal, then tie them in. Prune shoots that have flowered by making a cut above a healthy bud and removing about two thirds of their length. Also shorten any overlong stems that are spoiling the shape.

Pruning clematis

New clematis often benefit from being pruned back hard after planting. Prune out any dead, diseased or damaged growth, remove any weak stems, and cut back all the strong stems to healthy buds about 30cm (12in) above the ground. New growth produced the following year should be spaced out and tied into the support.

Once clematis are established, the pruning method depends on the type. There are three distinct groups:

Group 1 This includes the early-flowering types – *alpina*, *armandii*, *macropetala* and *montana* – that produce dainty blooms on old wood from midwinter to early spring. Unless they have outgrown their allotted space, most require little

Pruning a mid-season clematis (group 2)

In early spring, just as the growth buds start to swell, cut back all old stems to a strong, healthy pair of leaf buds. Remove any dead, weak or damaged stems.

Pruning a late-flowering clematis (group 3)

This clematis has outgrown its support and needs hard pruning in early spring; this will also improve flowering later in the year.
① First, tackle the abundant, tangled top-growth. Pull or cut it from the support so you can get a better idea of what is going on at the base.
② Cut back healthy stems to a strong pair of buds within 30cm (12in) of the soil level. Make your pruning cuts straight across the stems with sharp secateurs.

pruning other than the removal of dead, diseased or damaged stems after flowering. (*See also* page 78.)

Group 2 These clematis flower on old wood in late spring or early summer and often produce a second flush of blooms on new shoots in late summer. They include large-flowered varieties such as 'Nelly Moser', 'Vyvyan Pennell' and 'The President'. Cut back old stems to strong buds in early spring (*see* left). You can encourage a second flush of flowers by 'relay pruning' – after the first flush of flowers, cut half the stems back to a pair of healthy buds about 1m (40in) above ground level. (*See also* page 83.)

Group 3 These clematis flower from summer into autumn and include some of the large-flowered hybrids,

such as 'Jackmanii' and 'Perle d'Azur'. They need to be pruned routinely to keep them flowering well. In early spring, cut back all the stems to a pair of strong, healthy buds at about 30cm (12in) above soil level. (*See also* page 84.)

Early-flowering clematis, such as this montana type, require little pruning unless they outgrow their space.

Lonicera periclymenum 'Serotina' should be pruned immediately after flowering.

Pruning honeysuckles

Unless it has several strong stems, a new plant should be cut back by up to two thirds after planting. Tie in the strongest new shoots and remove any weak growth.

Pruning for more flowers

Honeysuckles can be divided into two pruning groups. Those bearing flowers in pairs on the new growth produced during the current season, including *Lonicera japonica* varieties (such as 'Halliana'), don't need routine pruning. However, you can cut them back in winter or early spring, removing some of the oldest stems near the base. This prevents all the flowers being produced out of sight at the top. Honeysuckles that produce flowers in whorls on old wood, including varieties of *Lonicera periclymenum* (such as 'Belgica'), should be pruned after flowering, with the flowered shoots cut back to a newer sideshoot lower down.

Pruning wisteria

In the first spring – or immediately after planting – cut out any dead, damaged or diseased growth (looking out for frost-damaged shoot-tips, which are quite common), and prune the tips of each shoot back to just above a strong, healthy bud. Space out and tie in the new growth to the support, to encourage an even coverage, cutting back any unwanted shoots to about 15cm (6in) in length. Tie in new growth throughout the growing season to establish a good framework.

Pruning for more flowers

Wisteria produces abundant leafy growth that needs regular trimming to keep it in check and producing flowers. It is best to prune in two stages. In late summer, cut back new whippy growth to five or six leaves; in winter, cut the same stems back to two or three buds. These flowering spurs will produce blooms the following spring. Any new shoots produced since the summer pruning should also be cut back.

How to prune wisteria

A mature wisteria will need pruning in two stages to keep it healthy and flowering successfully: the first stage takes place in late summer; the second stage involves more precise cuts and happens in late winter.

① In late summer, cut back all the current season's long, whippy stems to about 15–20cm (6–8in) using a pair of sharp secateurs. Tie in the remaining shoots until they begin to twine and to support themselves.

② In late winter, the shoots that you pruned in late summer should be pruned back to two or three buds. These are the spurs that will carry the flowers the following spring. At the same time, prune back any secondary growth – produced after the summer pruning – to 15–20cm (6–8in).

Pruning other popular climbers and wall shrubs

CLIMBERS	WHEN AND HOW TO PRUNE
Actinidia	Late winter or early spring; shorten extension growth by one third to a half.
Akebia (chocolate vine)	Late winter or early spring; shorten extension growth by one third.
Ampelopsis	Winter; shorten overlong growth to prevent it clogging up gutters.
Berberidopsis (coral plant)	Spring, after the last frost; cut out weak stems to thin out congested growth.
Billardiera (climbing blueberry)	Early spring or late summer, after flowering; cut back excessive growth to three buds.
Campsis (trumpet vine)	In late winter or early spring; shorten extension growth and cut back sideshoots to three buds.
Celastrus (oriental bittersweet, staff vine)	Only if necessary, in winter or early spring; shorten extension growth to three buds.
Clianthus	Only if necessary, after flowering; shorten overlong stems by up to one third.
Eccremocarpus (Chilean glory flower)	Spring; cut back extension growth to 30–60cm (1–2ft) of the base.
Hedera (ivy)	Early spring; cut excess growth back to keep gutters clear.
Humulus lupulus (hop)	Early spring (all shoots die back in winter); cut to ground level.
Hydrangea anomala subsp. *petiolaris* (climbing hydrangea)	After flowering; shorten wayward sideshoots and cut back excessive growth.
Jasminum (jasmine)	After flowering; cut back unwanted shoots to three buds.
Lathyrus latifolius (everlasting pea)	Spring; cut back last season's growth to near ground level.
Parthenocissus (Virginia creeper, Boston ivy)	Early winter; use shears to cut back excess growth and leave plenty of room for new growth.
Passiflora (passion flower)	Spring; remove any dead stems and thin out congested growth. After flowering, cut back extension growth to three buds.
Schisandra	Late winter or early spring; trim wayward growth to three buds.
Schizophragma (Japanese hydrangea vine)	Only if necessary, after flowering; cut back wayward shoots by two thirds.
Solanum (Chilean potato tree, potato vine)	Early spring; cut back excess growth and shorten sideshoots to three buds from the main stems.
Trachelospermum	Early spring; shorten wayward shoots and thin out congested growth.
Vitis (vine)	Midwinter; shorten sideshoots to three buds to form spurs.

WALL SHRUBS

Camellia	Only if necessary, after flowering; cut back unwanted stems to three buds. Dead-head after flowering.
Ceanothus (California lilac)	Prune autumn-flowering in spring; prune spring- and early summer-flowering after flowering. Prune previous season's growth by about one third.
Chaenomeles (flowering quince)	After flowering and again in summer; cut back sideshoots to three leaves to form flowering spurs.
Cotoneaster horizontalis	Late winter; remove wayward shoots.
Cytisus battandieri (pineapple broom)	Summer, after flowering; cut back exhausted growth to newer sideshoots lower down.
Garrya elliptica (silk-tassel bush)	Early spring, after flowering; remove wayward shoots.

Renovating overgrown plants

Old, neglected climbers and wall shrubs often become very woody at the base, and flower production declines. Any remaining flowers tend to be out of sight at the top of the plant, where all the new growth is produced, making the plant top-heavy and liable to collapse. Fortunately, many climbers and wall shrubs respond well to being cut back hard.

How to renovate a climber

Most neglected climbers can be pruned to encourage new, vigorous growth but only if they are still in fairly good condition. Renovation pruning of overgrown, tangled climbers is best carried out in stages, over a period of a few years. Cut out roughly one third of all the old stems each year, or concentrate on just one area and prune this back hard. After three or four years, the whole plant will have been rejuvenated.

Renovating wall shrubs

Wall shrubs that are essentially sound are worth renovating by cutting back; some, such as camellia

After renovation pruning, new growth that is produced on a wisteria will be strong and healthy.

and pyracantha, can be cut back hard. Most deciduous shrubs should be pruned while dormant (late autumn to early spring), but evergreens are best tackled just as they start to put on new growth (usually mid-spring). Many shrubs can be cut back hard to a knee-high, stubby framework. With a large specimen it's best to do this in two stages: first, remove all the major branches to clear the way; second, reduce the stumps to the right height. Where regrowth is vigorous, thin out crowded stems the following year.

If pruning the whole plant in one go is too drastic for you, try using the one-in-three method described for climbers (*see* left). Prune shrubs that flower on old wood after flowering; prune those that flower on current-season's growth in early spring.

Renovation techniques

CUT BACK ALMOST TO GROUND LEVEL

Ampelopsis	Cobaea scandens
Bougainvillea	Humulus lupulus
Campsis	Jasminum
Clematis, deciduous	Vitis

CUT BACK TO A STUBBY FRAMEWORK

Garrya elliptica	Parthenocissus
Hedera	Trachelospermum
Lonicera	Wisteria

CUT OUT ONE STEM IN THREE

Actinidia	Pileostegia viburnoides
Akebia	
Callistemon	Schizophragma hydrangeoides
Clematis, evergreen	Solanum
Hydrangea anomala subsp. petiolaris	Stauntonia

OLD CLIMBERS TO REPLACE

Dregea sinensis	Lathyrus
Eccremocarpus scaber	Mandevilla
	Passiflora
Hoya	Rhodochiton

HOW TO renovate a climber

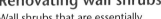

1 In late winter or early spring, prune out any dead, damaged or diseased growth then cut down a third to half of the remaining stems to ground level. After pruning, top-dress with a balanced fertilizer to promote the growth of strong, new stems.

2 During the following winter or in early spring, space new stems evenly over the support, untying if necessary. Shorten the tallest stems at the top of the support and cut down the remaining stems to 30cm (12in) above ground level.

It's not just sub-zero temperatures that are a threat to borderline-hardy plants. Wet winters and cold winds can also take their toll. Even some seemingly frost-proof plants may be at risk when they've just been planted, while normally robust plants may need extra protection in colder regions and within exposed gardens. Container plants are particularly at risk.

Climbing hydrangeas are fully hardy. Leave the lacy flowerheads on over winter; they look beautiful dusted with frost.

Wind damage

Cold, penetrating winds can damage all borderline-hardy climbers and wall shrubs, but it is evergreens that are most in danger. Minor damage can include scorched leaf-margins and exposed shoots, but in severe cases – and especially where plants are in containers – whole plants can be killed. You can protect individual climbers and wall shrubs that need shelter, such as *Abutilon*, *Callistemon*, *Carpenteria*,

evergreen ceanothus, *Fremontodendron californicum* and the less hardy jasmines, with a layer of windbreak netting fabric. In cold snaps, it's a good idea to insulate frost-tender plants by covering them with a winter 'duvet' made from a double layer of netting, stuffed with dry leaves or straw.

A few climbers, such as jasmine, passion flower and *Solanum*, will – if their tops are killed over the winter but their roots are protected – produce new shoots from below ground. The coldest weather is usually

between Christmas and Easter, so make sure you put down an insulating layer in plenty of time. The simplest method is to cover the root and crown with a layer of very dry material, such as autumn leaves, to a depth of about 15cm (6in).

Climbers in containers

Prolonged cold spells can freeze solid the rootball of a climber or wall shrub growing in a container. Protect individual vulnerable climbers and wall shrubs that are too big to move to a sheltered spot by parcelling up the whole plant. Using a waterproof insulating material, such as bubble polythene, wrap plenty of it around the container itself and then put a sleeve of double-thickness horticultural fleece over the whole plant.

You can insulate plants from frost in several ways.
① Wrap the container in bubble polythene and tie it in place with string.
② Place a mulch of dry autumn leaves over the crown of a climber or wall shrub.

Don't forget

Many vulnerable plants are easy to root from cuttings taken in late summer and early autumn. If you are unable to insulate a prized mature specimen, take cuttings as an insurance against any winter losses. It's worth doing this even if you do protect your plants over the winter months.

Propagation

Many climbers and wall shrubs are easy to propagate. Taking cuttings may seem the most obvious method, but because climbers have long, flexible stems, layering can be an easy alternative. Some climbers, such as wisteria, are tricky and best left to the professionals, but annual climbers are easily raised from seed.

Taking cuttings

There are various ways of taking cuttings. The two most often used are nodal and internodal. Nearly all climbers, including *Actinidia*, *Akebia*, *Campsis* and ivies, are propagated from nodal cuttings. Honeysuckle and jasmine can also be propagated from internodal cuttings, and these are the usual type for clematis.

A nodal cutting is normally taken from the tip of a shoot. Cut the stem straight across just below a leaf or pair of leaves (the node). Pinch out the fleshy growing-tip to encourage side-branching and prevent wilting. Remove the lower leaves before inserting the cutting into compost.

To make internodal cuttings, you cut the stem for the bottom of the cutting just above a bud (between nodes). The base of the cutting will be bare stem, with no buds or leaves. This is economical on plant material, as you may get several cuttings from a single trailing shoot. Cut through the stem about 1–2 cm (½–¾in)

Don't forget

Collect the material when the shoots are fresh and lively. Choose healthy-looking stems and remove flowers or flower buds.

above each node; you will then be left with a cutting that has a few centimetres of stem below each node and leaves, and a handy little stick above it. Varieties with more widely spaced nodes may need trimming, to produce cuttings around 11–13cm (4½–5in) long. Clematis cuttings are taken with just a single node, but this must have strong, undamaged growth buds nestled at the leaf bases. Push the

HOW TO take softwood cuttings

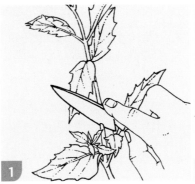

1 In spring cut several strong, healthy stems from the plant. Always use a clean, sharp knife. A cutting about 8cm (3in) long with two to three leaves at its tip works well for most plants. Take a few more than you need as an insurance policy.

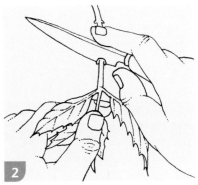

2 Pinch off the lowest leaves from each cutting and trim it just below a leaf-joint, or node (or just above, for internodal cuttings). You can dip the cuttings in hormone rooting powder, but this is not necessary.

3 Fill a pot with cutting compost mixed with a little sharp sand. Moisten well. Make holes in the compost with a dibber or a pencil and insert the cuttings around the edge. Make sure the leaves of adjacent cuttings don't touch each other.

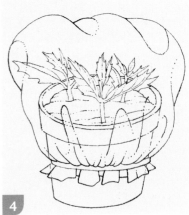

4 Cover the pot with a clear plastic bag, holding it in place with an elastic band. This mini-greenhouse will keep humidity high until the roots form. Pot up the cuttings when new growth starts (in about four to six weeks).

cutting right into the compost, so the leaves are just sitting on top.

Many wall shrubs, including pyracantha, are best propagated by heel cuttings – sideshoots pulled away from the main stem. These should be 10–15cm (4–6in) long and ideally without buds or flowers, so the plant puts its energy into making roots.

Nodal or internodal cuttings can be taken from soft or semi-ripe stems, and nodal cuttings from hard wood, depending partly on the time of year and partly on the plant you want to propagate. All should be rooted in cutting compost or multipurpose compost, with added sharp sand for drainage.

Softwood and semi-ripe cuttings

Softwood cuttings are made from the soft, new, current season's growth at the shoot-tips. They are usually taken early in the season and from plants that root easily. *Actinidia*, clematis, honeysuckle, ivy and jasmine can be propagated this way, as can most evergreen wall shrubs, including *Abutilon*, ceanothus and euonymus.

Semi-ripe cuttings are usually taken in late summer to autumn, when the shoots are still supple but have started to turn woody at the base. This type of cutting suits camellia, *Parthenocissus* and *Trachelospermum*. Semi-ripe cuttings take longer to root but, because the growth is not as soft, it is easier to keep the cuttings alive.

Hardwood cuttings

Some deciduous climbers, including *Campsis*, clematis, jasmine, roses and vines, can be propagated from hardwood cuttings taken in the dormant season. Choose a healthy-looking stem and make a straight cut at the bottom (just below a bud) and an angled cut at the top (just above a bud) – this will remind you later on which is the top. The length of the cutting will be around 15cm–20cm (6–8in). Some people dip the base of the cutting in hormone rooting powder or gel. Insert the cuttings in pots of multipurpose or cutting compost with sharp sand and place them in a cold frame or in a sheltered spot in the garden. Clematis may root better in a frost-free greenhouse.

Root cuttings

A few climbers, notably hops (*Humulus*) and perennial sweet pea (*Lathyrus*), can also be propagated from their roots. In winter, gently explore the soil around the base of a plant to expose the root system.

HOW TO take hardwood cuttings

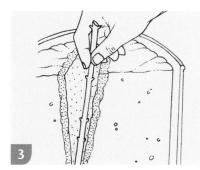

1

In the dormant season use sharp secateurs to cut a length of healthy stem from the current year's growth. Make a straight cut near the bottom, just below a bud.

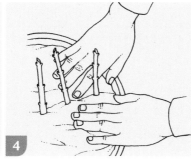

2

Make a sloping cut just above a bud at the top. The cutting should be about 15– 20cm (6–8in) long. If you want to, you can dip the base in hormone rooting powder.

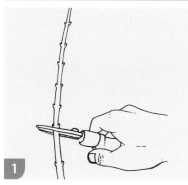

3

Fill a pot with cutting compost, adding sharp sand for drainage. Insert the cutting, base first, into a small slit trench you've made in the compost, leaving only the top third of the cutting showing above the surface.

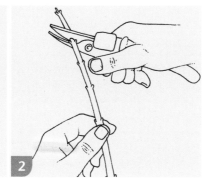

4

Add more cuttings to the trench then fill it in by firming compost all around it. Water the cuttings, then stand the pot in a cold frame or in a frost-free, sheltered spot outside over winter. Once the cuttings have rooted, pot them up.

Select thick, young, fleshy roots and cut them from the parent plant with a sharp knife. Make a straight cut at the end near the plant and an angled cut at the other end, so the prepared root cutting is about 5cm (2in) long. Insert the root cuttings vertically, flat end up, into multipurpose compost with added sharp sand and keep them in a warm place. Shoots should start to appear after a few weeks.

Layering

This is the easiest way to create one or two new plants from an existing plant, and a whole host of climbers and wall shrubs can be propagated in this way: *Campsis*, clematis, ivies, *Parthenocissus* and *Trachelospermum* all work well. Even if you are not sure, it's worth giving this a go.

Basically, you bend a vigorous, flexible shoot down to the ground and peg it into the soil. Then you wait for it to root and make another plant. The easiest way to secure the

shoot is to push a short, stout bamboo cane into the soil and tie the free end of the shoot securely to it where it emerges from the soil. This marks the spot where you have made the layer and supports your new plant when it has rooted.

Ivies, honeysuckles and winter jasmine will all 'self-layer', with

shoots rooting where sprawling stems touch the soil. Once well rooted, detach them, pot them up or plant them in their final position.

Growing sweet peas

The gardener's favourite annual climber, the sweet pea (*Lathyrus odoratus*) is a hardy annual and can be planted out early. Sweet pea experts sow seed in autumn and overwinter the young plants in cold frames, before planting out in early spring.

Whatever you read about the right way to raise sweet peas, they are easy to grow. Sow any time up to mid-spring indoors, and keep them as cool as possible and with plenty of light. Harden them off and then plant them out. The secret of success is to sow the seed in deep pots or tubes to encourage a deep root system, and pinch out the tips when the plants are around 8cm (3in) tall to encourage strong shoots to grow from the base. When you sow sweet peas, only grow scented ones, picking them often to encourage further production.

Don't forget

The best wisterias are grafted. This means that they are not growing on their own roots. Layering is unlikely to be successful with grafted plants.

HOW TO propagate a climber by layering

1 Look for a low-growing, healthy stem and, with the stem still attached to the plant, strip off the leaves about 20cm (8in) behind the growing-tip.

2 Bringing the stem down to ground level, bend it at right angles to form an 'elbow' and peg this into the ground about 20cm (8in) from the tip.

3 Insert a short bamboo cane next to the length of stem that isn't pegged down and tie it carefully to the bamboo cane with soft twine for support.

4 Firm down the soil around the layered stem and water thoroughly. When the layered cutting has rooted, detach it from the parent and pot it up.

Raising climbers from seed

Many annual climbers are easily raised from seed. Plants such as black-eyed Susan (*Thunbergia*), climbing nasturtium (*Tropaeolum*), cup-and-saucer vine (*Cobaea scandens*) and Chilean glory flower (*Eccremocarpus scaber*) can be sown indoors in late winter to early spring and kept somewhere warm to germinate, provided you have somewhere light and frost free to grow them on. They will need to stay there until it is safe to plant them outside in their final flowering position, once the threat of frost has passed. Short-lived perennial climbers such as morning glory (*Ipomoea*) are also propagated and grown on in the same way, from seed sown each year.

HOW TO raise annual climbers from seed

In early spring, fill a pot with seed compost then tap the bottom of the pot to settle it. Scatter the seed sparingly over the surface of the compost. Some seeds need a thin covering so add a layer of sieved compost. Stand the pot in tepid water until moisture has soaked all the way up to the surface of the compost.

Seeds germinate best in a warm, humid environment, so put them in a propagator or place a plastic bag over the pot and set it in a light spot out of direct sunlight. Check the seedlings to ensure the compost doesn't dry out. When the first seedlings appear take the covering off (raised lids can be left on) and remove any that are weak or damaged.

HOW TO prick out and pot up seedlings

First, have to hand a clean seed tray filled with fresh compost. Then take your pot of seedlings and use a dibber or a pencil to lift up clumps and loosen and separate the roots from the compost. Always handle seedlings by their leaves, never by the fragile stems, which are easily damaged.

Make holes in the compost about 3.5cm (1½in) apart and gently lower a seedling into each. Firm the compost around the seedlings then water them in, either by standing the tray in water or by using a small watering can with a very fine rose. Place the seedlings in a bright spot, but out of direct sunlight.

Keep seedlings moist but avoid overwatering. Once they have developed a pair of true leaves (the first leaves are called the 'seed leaves') you can pot them on into larger pots filled with fresh, sterilized compost. Keep the young plants in a light, frost-free place until the weather is warm enough to plant them out.

Plant problems and remedies

Fortunately, climbers and wall shrubs are generally not seriously threatened by pests and diseases. However, that doesn't mean they don't suffer from some of the same problems as other groups of plants. As always, prevention is better than cure. Pick a plant that's right for the position you have in mind and it could well show resistance to all but the most serious attacks.

You can reduce the impact of pest and disease problems by staying vigilant. If outbreaks are caught early they're much easier to deal with. All it takes is a walk around the garden in the evening, checking vulnerable climbers and wall shrubs. Individual pests, such as slugs, snails and caterpillars, can be picked off by hand and disposed of. Small colonies of aphids found in the soft growing-tips of clematis and other susceptible plants are also easy to squish between finger and thumb. Another way of limiting problems is to practise good garden hygiene. This means clearing up promptly – a garden doesn't have to be tidy, but it should be well kept.

Beneficial predators

One of the most effective ways of controlling pests is to encourage the natural predators that feed on them. You can do this by providing suitable habitats where these creatures can feed, breed and set up home. Nectar-rich flowers, for example, will attract hoverflies and lacewings, which eat aphids, spider mites and other insect pests, while piles of decomposing logs will provide a home for ground beetles and centipedes, which devour slugs and vine weevils. A small wildlife pond will soon be colonized by frogs and toads, who will scour your borders for slugs.

Common pests

Aphids

These small green or black sap-sucking insects attack roses and other climbers and can spread disease.

Prevention and control Squash them as soon as you see them or dislodge them with jets of water. Organic controls include insecticidal soap sprays. Attracting beneficial predators, such as lacewings, into your garden is always helpful.

Capsid bugs

Leaves at the shoot-tips of plants may be distorted, with small holes, when attacked by these sap-sucking pests. Flowers can be damaged in a similar way.

Prevention and control Keep your beds and borders well weeded and, if you have a major problem, spray with insecticide.

Caterpillars

These are butterfly and moth larvae, which hatch and feed on garden plants. Signs of attack are usually irregular holes eaten in leaves.

Prevention and control Pick off and squash caterpillars by hand.

Cut out stems and branches where colonies are feeding. If the problem is severe, consider using a biological control to limit their numbers.

Earwigs

During the summer months, earwigs have a tendency to destroy flowers, particularly clematis, by cutting holes in and shredding petals. They are night feeders, so you are likely to see them only by torchlight.

Prevention and control Trap earwigs in upturned pots filled with straw on top of short canes (these imitate flowers) or rolled up pieces of corrugated cardboard. Simply empty the traps in the morning.

Flea beetles

The leaves of potato vine and Chilean potato tree (*Solanum*) peppered with holes – as if they have been attacked with a shotgun – are sure signs of flea-beetle damage. The beetles become active during dry spells in spring, so a climber against a sheltered wall is a prime target.

Prevention and control Remove badly damaged foliage and feed and water all climbers against walls during dry spells to encourage strong growth.

Leaf miners

The grubs of these tiny flies create chambers and tunnels under the surface of leaves. Damage is common on many plants, especially pyracantha and Russian vine (*Fallopia baldschuanica*). If plants are healthy and growing strongly they can tolerate attacks without suffering any real damage.

Prevention and control Pick off and destroy any affected leaves as soon as you notice them.

Leaf-rolling sawfly

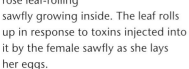

This pest specifically attacks roses. If you see rose leaflets rolled tightly and hanging down, unroll them and you will find the pale green grub of the rose leaf-rolling sawfly growing inside. The leaf rolls up in response to toxins injected into it by the female sawfly as she lays her eggs.

Prevention and control Only one generation of eggs hatches per year – during the summer – so pick off affected leaves and you may eradicate the problem for that year at least. Keep the soil under plants well weeded in winter to expose overwintering larvae to predators.

Red spider mite

In sheltered parts of the garden, especially during warm weather, spider mites can infest the foliage of several climbers including clematis,

jasmine, sweet pea, trumpet vine (*Campsis*) and wisteria. Signs to look out for are mottled, yellow leaves and fine webbing.

Prevention and control Increase humidity around plants during dry spells and consider using a biological control during the summer months. If damage is severe, spray with a suitable insecticide.

Scale insects

These sap-suckers attack the foliage and stems of many wall shrubs and climbers. When they feed, some types of scale insect excrete a sticky honeydew. This can become colonized by black sooty mould, which also harms the plant.

Prevention and control Pick or scrub off minor infestations and use barrier glue around plant stems. Apply a biological control to limit numbers or spray with an insecticide in early summer, when the larvae are on the move.

Slugs and snails

Look out for nibbled leaves, stripped foliage and slime trails, especially around clematis and sweet peas – plants that these troublesome creatures find particularly attractive to graze on.

Prevention and control Protect vulnerable plants, including seedlings and emerging new shoots, with barriers of grit or collars made from copper or cut-down plastic drinks bottles. Pick off the pests by torchlight and set beer traps (remembering to empty them). You can also apply a biological control containing nematodes.

Thrips

These slim-line, sap-sucking insects feed on the upper surface of honeysuckle and sweet-pea leaves and flowers, causing silvery flecking. The light flecking later turns brown.

Prevention and control Keep plants well watered and spray with an organic pesticide based on plant extracts, such as pyrethrum.

Vine weevils

Particularly troublesome on camellias and *Euonymus*, the adult weevils disfigure foliage, munching notches out of the edges of leaves. Their cream-coloured, brown-headed grubs feed unseen on plant roots.

Prevention and control Collect up the adults at night by torchlight to prevent them from breeding. Encourage natural predators such as birds, frogs, toads, hedgehogs and ground beetles. If the problem is severe, apply a biological control.

Common diseases

As with garden pests, the best way of tackling diseases is prevention. Where possible, choose disease-resistant varieties when you are buying new plants. This is particularly important with climbers, such as roses, that habitually suffer from the same problems. Keeping your plants healthy and giving them the site, soil and conditions they prefer will also go a long way towards helping them fight off common diseases.

Botrytis

Also known as grey mould because of its fuzzy appearance on parts of the plant above ground, this common fungus

may attack flowering quince (*Chaenomeles*), jasmine, *Solanum* and roses. It usually gains entry after pest damage to flowers or fruits, and causes them to rot.

Prevention and control
Prune out diseased stems and leaves and burn them. Also make sure there is good air circulation around wall shrubs and climbers. Dead-head plants regularly.

Coral spot

Keep a look out for this fungal disease. It attacks old or dead stems of woody plants and shows up as pink or reddish-orange spots.

Pyracantha and wisteria may suffer from it. The fungus can spread from dead wood to healthy growth.

Prevention and control
Prune out all affected stems and make sure you clean the blades of your tools to prevent the disease spreading to other plants. Burn infected wood.

Downy mildew

Upper leaf surfaces develop yellow or brown areas, and there is grey or purplish mould on the undersides. This disease is a particular nuisance on camellias, clematis, honeysuckle, ivy, *Parthenocissus*, *Solanum*, *Tropaeolum* and wisteria. On mature climbers and wall shrubs, badly affected leaves die, but the plant itself may not be severely affected.

Prevention and control Improve air circulation around established shrubs and climbers by careful pruning. Give new plants plenty of space.

Fireblight

If this bacterial disease is present, the flowering stems of cotoneaster and pyracantha turn brown at the tips, as if scorched. It enters through the flowers and spreads up the stem, eventually killing the whole plant.

Prevention and control
Cut out all affected stems promptly and make sure you clean the blades of your tools. There is no chemical control so it's best to grow resistant varieties, such as the *Pyracantha* 'Saphyr' range.

Honey fungus

This deadly disease of woody plants has been known to affect camellias, ceanothus and wisteria. Plants

may produce a bumper crop of flowers just before dying back. Honey-coloured toadstools may grow around the affected plant.

Prevention and control Dig up and burn affected plants and remove the surrounding soil. *Carpenteria*, flowering quince, clematis and passion flower appear to show some resistance to this disease.

Leaf spots, including black spot

As the name suggests, spots develop on the leaves of climbers including clematis, honeysuckle, ivy and wisteria as well as wall shrubs such as camellia. Few leaf spots are fatal. The exception is rose black spot, but this can often be prevented by growing resistant varieties.

Prevention and control
Prune out affected leaves and clear up and burn infected leaves at the end of the season so that the disease

cannot carry over into spring and affect new foliage. Mulching will also help prevent the spores in the soil infecting new foliage.

Powdery mildew

White powdery deposits appear on the leaves, stems and flower buds of clematis, honeysuckle, roses and sweet peas. Plants can become stunted and even die in severe mildew attacks.

Prevention and control
Powdery mildew thrives in dry conditions, so water plants well in dry spells, especially those growing near walls and fences, but avoid splashing the leaves. Prune out affected shoots. Apply sulphur dust, which is an organic control, or, if necessary, a suitable fungicide.

Rust

Brown or rust-coloured spots develop on the underside of leaves as well as stems. This fungal disease can affect several climbers, notably honeysuckle and roses.

Prevention and control
You can stop rust taking hold by improving and increasing air circulation around your wall shrubs and climbers. Thin out overcrowded stems and give plants plenty of space. Pick off affected leaves and rake up diseased leaves in autumn. Dispose of them; don't add them to the compost heap.

Clematis wilt

If one or more of the shoots on your clematis suddenly wilts and even dies, this troublesome fungal disease may be to blame. The disease spreads from the leaves into the leaf-stalks and stem. Sap cannot pass through the infected tissue, which turns black, and the stem above it dies. If there is no other obvious cause, such as a lack of water, cut the affected stems back to healthy tissue – this may mean cutting right back to ground level. With luck, new healthy shoots will be produced the following spring, especially if you planted the clematis deeply, with any dormant buds just below the surface.

The following species are resistant to wilt: *C. alpina, C. armandii, C. cirrhosa, C. macropetala, C. montana, C. texensis, C. tibetana* subsp. *vernayi, C. viticella.*

Other problems

FROST DAMAGE
The buds and flowers of camellias can be badly damaged by frost if they are planted in a spot that gets early morning sunshine straight after a very cold night. Plant camellias, especially the white varieties, by a shady wall where their beautiful flowers can emerge without coming to any harm.

IRON DEFICIENCY
Also called lime-induced chlorosis, this deficiency shows itself as yellowing of the foliage, starting at the edge of the leaf and then developing between the veins. It commonly affects acid-loving plants, such as camellias, that have been planted in soils that are too alkaline. Make sure that plants have the right soil, growing them in a pot of ericaceous compost if necessary. You can also buy iron compounds that you dissolve in water and apply to affected plants. Mulching them with chopped bracken or pine needles also helps.

PYRACANTHA SCAB
Brownish-green patches develop on affected leaves, which often become puckered and may fall prematurely. Flowers and berries also develop scabby patches. The disease is easy to confuse with fireblight (*see* opposite) and is worse in cool, damp summers. Prune out affected shoots and promptly clear away any fallen leaves. It is a good idea to grow resistant varieties of pyracantha, such as 'Navajo' and 'Orange Charmer', or the 'Saphyr' range, all of which appear to show some resistance to the disease.

ROSE REPLANT PROBLEMS
It often used to be the case that a new rose planted in a space where another had died would survive only if you removed and replaced all the old soil. Happily, rose replant disease can easily be overcome now by using a preparation of friendly mycorrhizal fungi.

SILVER LEAF
Although most commonly associated with cherries and plums (*Prunus*), this fungal disease can affect individual stems of honeysuckles, causing the leaves to turn silvery. The fungus usually gains entry through wounds caused by pests or as a result of pruning cuts. Prune out affected stems and clean the blades of your tools thoroughly to try to prevent the disease from spreading.

VIRUSES
Signs of virus attack are usually stunted or distorted growth and yellowing or white-streaked leaves. Remove and burn affected plants immediately, clear away nearby weeds and disinfect tools. If possible, always buy certified virus-free plants.

Recommended climbers and wall shrubs

One of the most versatile and decorative groups of garden plants, climbers are invaluable for adding height and colour to borders, softening hard outlines with foliage, or introducing a focal point when grown up an arch or through an existing tree. Wall shrubs add structure to the garden and make attractive features. Some display beautiful autumn berries and others, such as camellias, bear exquisite flowers in white, pink and deepest red.

A–Z directory

Whether you're looking for a colourful flowering screen or a shrub to add interest to a shady courtyard wall, there's a plant to fit the bill. Always take into account the conditions your garden offers so you choose the right plant for the right place.

Many climbers and wall shrubs have more than one season of interest, so offer outstanding value. Some climbers, however, can be very vigorous and it pays to check the plant's eventual height and spread so it won't outgrow the location you have in mind. For other climber and wall shrub recommendations, *see* Plants for a purpose, pages 40–1.

KEY to symbols

In this chapter the following symbols are used to indicate a plant's preferred growing conditions. A rough idea is also given as to what each plant's height (H) and spread (S) might be at maturity.

Unless otherwise specified, plants are fully hardy and deciduous.

○ Prefers/tolerates an open, sunny site

◐ Prefers/tolerates some shade

● Prefers/tolerates full shade

❄ Will survive winter in a sheltered site

❀ Always needs protection from frost

◗ Prefers/tolerates moist soil

◌ Prefers/tolerates dry soil

⇊ Needs well-drained soil

pH↓ Needs/prefers acidic soil

pH↑ Needs/prefers alkaline soil

pH→ Needs/prefers neutral soil

🍂 Needs humus-rich soil

❖ Season of main interest (e.g. flowers, foliage, stems, berries)

Abeliophyllum distichum
White forsythia

○ ❄ ⇊ ❖LATE WINTER or EARLY SPRING
H and S 1.5m (5ft)

Tiny, sweetly scented, pinkish-white, star-shaped flowers are produced *en masse* in late winter or early spring on purple-tinged, leafless stems. This shrub does best against a warm wall. Good variety: Roseum Group (white flowers flushed pink).

Abutilon megapotamicum
Trailing abutilon

○ ❄ ⇊ ❖SUMMER to AUTUMN
H and S 2m (6ft)

This lax, evergreen shrub has slender stems with eye-catching, red and yellow pendent lanterns. In milder areas, grow it against a sheltered wall for a tropical look and to show off the flowers to best advantage. It also makes an unusual container plant for the patio.

Acacia dealbata Mimosa

○ ❀ ⇊ pH→ −pH↓ ❖MIDWINTER to SPRING
H 15m (49ft) S 6m (20ft)

Although a full-blown tree in its native Australia, it won't reach its full potential in the UK. Sweetly scented, fluffy yellow, ball-shaped flowers smother the tips of the silvery branches from midwinter to mid-spring, and its ferny evergreen foliage is also attractive. Try it in a large container in a conservatory or against a sheltered wall outside in mild areas.

Actinidia kolomikta

○ ⇊ ❖SPRING to SUMMER, AUTUMN
H 5m (16ft) S 4m (13ft)

This relative of the kiwi fruit is grown for its spectacular white-tipped foliage that matures to pink, as if each leaf has been dipped in paint. Pleasantly scented flowers are borne during early summer, followed by edible oval fruits produced on female plants. The foliage of this climber will clothe a sunny wall and make a splendid long-lasting feature.

Akebia quinata Chocolate vine
○ ◑ ◍ ↕ ❖SPRING, AUTUMN

H 10m (33ft) S 2m (6ft)

Once established, this dainty, semi-evergreen climber bears clusters of spicy, chocolate-scented, wine-red spring flowers against a backdrop of bright green foliage that becomes purple-flushed in colder weather. If the summer is long and warm you will also get a crop of unusual, sausage-shaped seedpods. Use it to cover an arch or pergola so that the flowers can be viewed from below.

Ampelopsis megalophylla
○ ◑ ◍ ↕ ❖LATE SUMMER, EARLY AUTUMN

H 10m (33ft) S 6m (20ft)

This is a lush-looking, large-leaved vine, with divided leaves that colour beautifully in autumn. Inconspicuous green flowers appear in late summer, followed by strange-looking, black fruits that resemble spinning tops. Grow it in a sunny spot and restrict the roots to get a reasonable quantity of berries.

Berberidopsis corallina
Coral plant
◑ ❄ pH→ −pH↓ ❖SUMMER

H 5m (16ft) S 2m (6ft)

The coral plant is an unusual, woody, evergreen climber clothed in large, heart-shaped, dark green leaves. Throughout summer the gracefully arching shoots carry pendent strings of ruby-red flowers in clusters, right to the tips. For a partially shaded, sheltered wall or fence that isn't in a frost pocket, this is an excellent choice.

Ampelopsis brevipedunculata var. maximowiczii 'Elegans'
○ ◑ ◍ ↕ ❖SUMMER, AUTUMN

H 5m (16ft) S 1m (40in)

This underrated climber will add interest to any size of garden. Its pink, cream and green mottled leaves have flesh-pink tendrils that give the plant an alien appearance. In long, warm summers you will also be able to enjoy its unusual, gemstone-like, turquoise berries. It is ideal for growing up trellis or an obelisk or wigwam in a container.

Aristolochia macrophylla
Dutchman's pipe
○ ◑ ↕ ❖SUMMER

H 10m (33ft) S 8m (26ft)

The unusual flowers of this strong-growing, twining climber are tubular with ends that open out and curve upwards, like an old-fashioned pipe. Yellow-green in colour and mottled, the flowers appear among large, heart-shaped leaves. Grow this attractive climber up a high wall, using wires.

Billardiera longiflora
Climbing blueberry
○ ◑ ❄ pH→ −pH↓ 🌿 ❖SUMMER, AUTUMN

H and S 2m (6ft)

Everybody who sees this evergreen, twining climber wants to take it home. Amazing deep-purple, red, pink or white, pepper-shaped fruits up to 2cm (¾in) long dangle on wiry stems like Christmas-tree decorations and follow on from bell-shaped, green summer flowers. It needs a sheltered position and prefers dappled shade, but will take direct sun.

Callistemon citrinus 'Splendens'
Crimson bottlebrush

○ ❄ ⇊ pH→ –pH↓ ❖ SPRING, SUMMER
H 2m (6ft) S 1.5m (5ft)

An alluring container shrub for the patio
or conservatory, this plant becomes the
centre of attention in spring and
summer, when exotic-looking, crimson,
bottlebrush-like flower spikes appear at
the tips of lax, arching branches. The
evergreen foliage releases a lemon scent
when rubbed. Grow it in mild coastal
gardens or against a south-facing wall.

Camellia japonica
Common camellia

◑ ◖ pH↓ 🍃 ❖ SPRING
H 9m (30ft) S 8m (26ft)

The spectacular, mid- to late-spring
flowers on this vigorous evergreen shrub
with lustrous leaves resemble waterlilies.
Plant it against a wall in partial shade,
provided it doesn't catch the early
morning sun, which will damage the
flowers after a frost. Good varieties
(both smaller than C. japonica): 'Elegans'
(dark rose-pink flowers; shown above);
'Adolphe Audusson' (dark red flowers).

Camellia × williamsii
◑ ◖ pH↓ 🍃 ❖ SPRING
H 5m (16ft) S 3m (10ft)

Showy, waxy-looking, white to dark pink
flowers are borne from mid- to late
spring on a rounded, evergreen shrub
with lustrous leaves. It is ideal for
planting against a wall in partial shade,
as long as it does not receive early
morning sun in spring, which will
damage any frosted flowers. Good
varieties: 'Anticipation' (crimson flowers);
'E.G. Waterhouse' (double, soft-pink
flowers; shown above); 'Debbie'
(rose-pink, peony-shaped flowers).

Campsis grandiflora
Chinese trumpet vine

○ ❄ ◖ ⇊ ❖ LATE SUMMER
H and S 10m (33ft)

Spectacular, trumpet-shaped, fiery late-
summer flowers in shades of orange and
red glow against the dark green foliage
of this vigorous, deciduous climber. It is
perfect for covering a large wall or fence
in a sheltered spot in full sun. Tie it into
its support at regular intervals.

Campsis radicans 'Flamenco'
○ ◑ ❄ ⇊ ❖ LATE SUMMER to EARLY AUTUMN
H and S 10m (33ft)

Clusters of slender, trumpet-shaped,
yellow flowers are produced on this
climber during late summer and early
autumn. It is ideal either for scrambling
through an established tree or to cover
a sheltered, sunny, vertical surface.
Although frost hardy, it does need
shelter from cold winds, so avoid
north-facing walls and fences.

Campsis × tagliabuana
'Madame Galen'

○ ❄ ◖ ⇊ ❖ LATE SUMMER
H and S 10m (33ft)

Producing splendid, fiery orange-red,
trumpet-shaped flowers during late
summer, this popular variety of trumpet
vine is the perfect addition to a sunny
wall or fence for a tropical look. This
woody climber also offers a cloak of
divided, dark green leaves that make
a good backdrop for earlier-flowering
plants. It is vigorous and will need
regular tying into its support.

Carpenteria californica 'Ladhams' Variety'

Tree anemone
○ ❄ ⇅ ❖ SUMMER
H and S 2m (6ft)

This stylish, evergreen shrub makes an eye-catching display from early to midsummer, trained against a sheltered wall or fence. The large, fragrant, white flowers, each with a golden boss of stamens, shine out against a backdrop of glossy, dark green leaves. It will need protection from cold winds.

Ceanothus arboreus 'Trewithen Blue' California lilac

○ ❄ ⇅ ❖ SPRING to EARLY SUMMER
H 6m (20ft) S 8m (26ft)

This large, spreading, evergreen shrub has fragrant, mid-blue flowers. Having an open habit, it does not catch the eye in quite the same way as other more compact forms, but the individual flower clusters are much larger (up to 12cm/5in long). Although hardy, this ceanothus does best at the back of a south- or west-facing shrub border or against a sunny wall, where it will be protected from winter winds.

Ceanothus 'Autumnal Blue'

California lilac
○ ❄ ⇅ ❖ LATE SUMMER to AUTUMN
H and S 3m (10ft)

Broccoli-like, fluffy clusters of intensely blue flowers are borne from late summer and last into the autumn. The flowers are produced in such numbers that the whole shrub seems to turn a vivid blue. Although hardy, this upright evergreen produces the best displays if given a sheltered site with protection from cold winter winds.

Ceanothus × delileanus 'Gloire de Versailles' California lilac

○ ❄ ⇅ ❖ MIDSUMMER to AUTUMN
H 1.5m (5ft) S 2m (6ft)

Deservedly popular, this deciduous California lilac forms a bushy shrub that's smothered in powder-blue flower clusters from midsummer to autumn. In cold areas, grow it at the edge of a south- or west-facing shrub border or against a south- or west-facing, sunny, sheltered wall where it will get some protection from damaging winter winds.

Celastrus orbiculatus

Oriental bittersweet, Staff vine
○ ◐ ⇅ ❖ AUTUMN
H 14m (45ft) S 4–6m (13–20ft)

This is a vigorous climber, with rounded, scalloped, mid-green leaves that have toothed edges and turn butter yellow in autumn. At this time, yellow seed capsules split to reveal glistening pink and scarlet fruits. The flowers are insignificant and produced in summer. It is ideal for covering large walls or for scrambling through an established tree.

Chaenomeles speciosa

Flowering quince
○ ◐ ◐ ⇅ ❖ SPRING to EARLY SUMMER, AUTUMN
H 2.5m (8ft) S 5m (16ft)

This vigorous wall shrub carries striking, scarlet spring flowers that last until early summer, on spiny branches. It is a particularly useful shrub for adding spring colour to east- and west-facing walls and fences. Aromatic, yellow-green fruits are produced in autumn. Good varieties (smaller than C. speciosa): 'Geisha Girl' (apricot-pink flowers); 'Moerloosei' (apple-blossom-pink flowers); 'Nivalis' (white flowers).

Clematis 'Abundance'
○ ◐ ‖ ❖SUMMER to AUTUMN

H 3m (10ft) S 1m (40in)

Dazzling wine-red cupped flowers, with pink and white veins and creamy anthers, are produced in succession from midsummer into autumn. A small-flowered clematis – its flowers are 5cm (2in) across – it is easy to grow and ideal for an inexperienced gardener. It does particularly well against fences and walls in sun or dappled shade. Pruning group 3 (see page 84).

Clematis 'Alba Luxurians'
○ ◐ ‖ ❖SUMMER to AUTUMN

H 4m (13ft) S 1.5m (5ft)

Flowering in late summer, this clematis has small, open bell-shaped, green-tipped white blooms with contrasting deep-purple centres, held over greyish-green foliage. This is a good choice for scrambling through an established tree or hedge. Pruning group 3 (see page 84).

Clematis 'Apple Blossom'
○ ◐ ❄ ‖ ❖EARLY SPRING

H 3m (10ft) S 2m (6ft)

Dainty, pink-flushed white, early-spring flowers that open white, with a lovely almond scent, are produced in massed clusters. They stand out beautifully against a backdrop of glossy, evergreen leaves. Although it is frost hardy, this clematis does need shelter from cold winter winds, so avoid planting it against north-facing walls and fences. Pruning group 1 (see page 78).

Clematis 'Arabella'
○ ◐ ‖ ❖LATE SUMMER to AUTUMN

H 2m (6ft) S 1m (40in)

This striking climber produces beautiful, iridescent, mauve-blue flowers that fade gracefully to light blue during late summer and into autumn. It is a compact, non-clinging, herbaceous clematis, and is ideal either for providing unusual ground cover between established shrubs or for growing up a wigwam in a container on the patio. It is an excellent choice where space is limited. Pruning group 3 (see page 84).

Clematis armandii 'Snowdrift'
○ ◐ ❄ ‖ ❖EARLY SPRING

H 3m (10ft) S 2m (6ft)

Gorgeous, star-shaped, creamy-white flowers, with a lovely almond fragrance, stand out against a backdrop of glossy, evergreen leaves in early spring. Although frost hardy, this variety will need shelter from cold winds, so north-facing walls and fences aren't suitable planting sites. Pruning group 1 (see page 78).

Clematis 'Barbara Jackman'
○ ◐ ‖

❖LATE SPRING to EARLY SUMMER, EARLY AUTUMN

H 2.5m (8ft) S 1m (40in)

A wonderful, large-flowered hybrid, this clematis bears striking, magenta-striped, mauve-blue blooms that seem to glow in the evening light. It flowers from late spring into early summer and again in early autumn. Compact and free-flowering, it makes an excellent container climber. Give it a deep, generous-sized pot, feed and water well and try to keep its roots in the shade. Pruning group 2 (see page 83).

Early-flowering clematis: pruning group 1

The delicate flowers of early clematis bring cheer and colour to the garden from midwinter through to early spring. Fragrant, evergreen species, such as *Clematis armandii*, offer particularly good value and the scent is sweet and uplifting.

Some of the early-flowering clematis, such as the Montana types, are very vigorous and make short work of covering a fence or an unpromising-looking garden shed. Scented varieties are ideal for planting against a sheltered wall near the house so you can appreciate their wonderful fragrance as soon as you step outside.

Clematis can be divided into three pruning groups. Early-flowering clematis are in the first group and produce flowers on old wood that has ripened the previous year; they include varieties of *Clematis alpina*, *C. armandii*, *C. macropetala* and *C. montana*. (For pruning groups 2 and 3, *see* pages 83 and 84.)

Clematis montana varieties are incredibly vigorous, early-flowering climbers that can quickly clothe a large expanse of wall or fence.

How and when to prune

Most early-flowering (group 1) clematis need little pruning, unless they have outgrown their allotted space. After flowering, remove any dead or damaged stems as well as those that are overlong and spoiling the shape of the plant. This will encourage the plant to form new growth that will produce flowers the following spring.

> **EARLY-FLOWERING VARIETIES**
> *Clematis* 'Apple Blossom'
> *C. armandii* 'Snowdrift'
> *C.* 'Early Sensation'
> *C.* 'Frankie'
> *C. macropetala* 'Lagoon'
> *C. macropetala* 'Wesselton'
> *C.* 'Markham's Pink'
> *C.* 'Willy'

As its name suggests, *Clematis* 'Early Sensation' is a dazzling climber that heralds the spring.

Clematis 'Bees' Jubilee'
○ ◐ ⬆⬆ ❖ SPRING to EARLY SUMMER, LATE SUMMER
H 2.5m (8ft) S 1m (40in)

This pretty, large-flowered hybrid bears dark pink flowers, which become more eye-catching as they fade to candyfloss pink with a deeper-pink, central stripe. It flowers from late spring into early summer and again in late summer. It produces flowers on the previous year's shoots, then on the tips of new shoots. Compact and free-flowering, it is good for a container. Pruning group 2 (*see* page 83).

Clematis 'Betty Corning'
○ ◐ ⬆⬆ ❖ MIDSUMMER to MID-AUTUMN
H 2m (6ft) S 1m (40in)

A continuous succession of charming, pale lilac, bell-shaped, subtly fragrant flowers are produced from midsummer to mid-autumn on this late, small-flowered climber. It is a good choice for growing either through established shrubs or over a hedge; make sure you cut it back each spring so it never outgrows its space. This is an ideal clematis for a small garden. Pruning group 3 (*see* page 84).

Clematis 'Bill MacKenzie'
○ ◐ ‖ ❖MIDSUMMER to EARLY AUTUMN, WINTER

H 7m (23ft) S 3m (10ft)

The fleshy-looking, rich yellow petals that form open bell-shaped blooms on this climber look a bit like pieces of orange peel. The flowers are produced in abundance from summer into autumn and are followed by fluffy seedheads that look great in autumn and winter. A fairly vigorous plant, it's a good choice for growing up an arch or over a pergola. Pruning group 3 (*see* page 84).

Clematis 'Black Prince'
○ ◐ ‖ ❖MIDSUMMER to EARLY AUTUMN

H 3m (10ft) S 1m (40in)

The sumptuous, dark purple flowers of this late-blooming clematis look nearly black in the fading light at the end of the day. The flowers are produced from summer to autumn. It's a particularly good choice for partnering roses, because you can cut it back each spring at the same time as you prune the roses. Pruning group 3 (*see* page 84).

Clematis cirrhosa var. balearica
○ ◐ ❄ ‖ ❖WINTER

H 2.5m (8ft) S 1.5m (5ft)

You'll need to get right up close to this bronze-tinted, evergreen clematis to appreciate the intricate, reddish-maroon freckling inside the fragrant, creamy-white, cup-shaped flowers. Although frost hardy, it needs shelter from cold winds. Plant it next to a doorway or arch it over a well-used path so that the winter flowers can be seen at close quarters and you can enjoy their scent. Pruning group 1 (*see* opposite).

Clematis cirrhosa var. purpurascens 'Freckles'
○ ◐ ❄ ‖ ❖WINTER to EARLY SPRING

H 3m (10ft) S 2m (6ft)

Just when the garden needs a lift, this delightful winter-flowering clematis produces a succession of fragrant, bell-shaped, creamy flowers. They are so heavily speckled inside with reddish-brown 'freckles', they can appear pink against a backdrop of glossy, evergreen leaves. Provide shelter from cold winds and don't plant against north-facing walls. Pruning group 1 (*see* opposite).

Clematis 'Comtesse de Bouchaud'
○ ◐ ‖ ❖MIDSUMMER to LATE SUMMER

H 2m (6ft) S 1m (40in)

This easy-to-grow, late-flowering variety produces single, brilliant mauve-pink blooms with contrasting golden anthers. A popular variety, it produces flowers in mid- and late summer. It is a strong-growing plant that looks stunning scrambling through established shrubs, as well as up an obelisk in the border. Pruning group 3 (*see* page 84).

Clematis 'Confetti'
○ ◐ ‖ ❖MIDSUMMER to MID-AUTUMN

H 3m (10ft) S 1m (40in)

Nodding, rich pink, splayed bell-shaped flowers are produced in succession from midsummer to mid-autumn against a curtain of fresh green leaves. Grow this clematis against a wall or fence, train it up an arch, or use it to cover an obelisk in the border. Pruning group 3 (*see* page 84).

Clematis 'Crystal Fountain'

○ ◑ ⚌ ❖ LATE SPRING to SUMMER

H and S 2m (6ft)

This unusual clematis, with striking, double, large, lavender-blue flowers, is distinguished by a dramatic ruff of greenish-white stamens. It flowers from late spring into early summer and it may sometimes flower again in late summer. Compact and free-flowering, it makes an excellent climber for a large container, given appropriate support. Pruning group 2 (*see* page 83).

Clematis 'Duchess of Albany'

○ ◑ ⚌ ❖ MIDSUMMER to MID-AUTUMN

H 2.5m (8ft) S 1.5m (5ft)

Outward-facing, tulip-shaped, deep-pink flowers with a darker central stripe are produced from summer to autumn. This clematis can take a few years to get established before it will flower, but it is well worth the wait. Grow it either against a wall or fence, or as an unusual flowering ground-cover plant, between established shrubs. Pruning group 3 (*see* page 84).

Clematis × durandii

○ ◑ ⚌ ❖ MIDSUMMER to EARLY AUTUMN

H 2.5m (8ft) S 1.5m (5ft)

This delightful, non-clinging climber bears moody, dark indigo-blue flowers, each with an eye made up of distinctive yellow anthers, from midsummer until early autumn. A compact climber, it's ideal for tying into a wigwam in a pot on the patio. It is also an excellent choice for a small garden, where space is limited. Pruning group 3 (*see* page 84).

Clematis 'Doctor Ruppel'

○ ◑ ⚌ ❖ LATE SPRING to SUMMER, AUTUMN

H 2.5m (8ft) S 1m (40in)

Masses of dark rose-pink flowers with a darker stripe and spidery, pale brown anthers are borne against a backdrop of fresh green foliage. It flowers from late spring into early summer and again in early autumn. The attractive flowers of this clematis tend not to fade or bleach in the sun, so it is a really good choice for a south-facing spot in the garden or on the patio. Pruning group 2 (*see* page 83).

Clematis 'Duchess of Edinburgh'

○ ◑ ⚌ ❖ LATE SPRING to SUMMER, AUTUMN

H 4m (13ft) S 2m (6ft)

If you need a partner for a climbing rose that you've trained up a trellis or an arch, this could be the perfect clematis. Its cool, double, white flowers, each with a warm yellow eye, will add charm and sophistication to your display. The flowers appear from late spring into early summer and may sometimes reappear in early autumn. Pruning group 2 (*see* page 83).

Clematis 'Elizabeth'

○ ◑ ⚌ ❖ LATE SPRING to EARLY SUMMER

H 7m (23ft) S 3m (10ft)

A much-loved, candyfloss-pink, late spring flowering clematis, it bears masses of sweetly scented, cross-shaped flowers, with pronounced golden anthers. They stand out beautifully against a backdrop of purple-tinged foliage. Grow it over an arch on a much-used path or next to an entrance so you can fully appreciate the lovely almond fragrance every time you pass. Pruning group 3 (*see* page 84).

Clematis 'Ernest Markham'
○ ‖ ❖LATE SUMMER
H 4m (13ft) S 1m (40in)

This lovely, vigorous clematis will be positively smothered in large, rich magenta flowers, each with a creamy-brown eye, in late summer. It is a sun-lover, so a climbing rose trained on a south-facing, sunny wall or fence would make an ideal companion. Pruning group 3 (*see* page 84).

Clematis 'Etoile Violette'
○ ◐ ‖ ❖MIDSUMMER to EARLY AUTUMN
H 3m (10ft) S 1.5m (5ft)

This free-flowering clematis looks sensational from summer to autumn, when it bears masses of cream-eyed, violet-purple blooms. It is a fairly vigorous clematis and makes a good choice for growing up an arch or covering a pergola. Pruning group 3 (*see* page 84).

Clematis 'Fireworks'
○ ◐ ‖ ❖LATE SPRING to SUMMER, AUTUMN
H 4m (13ft) S 2m (6ft)

Brightly coloured and extremely eye-catching, the large, two-tone flowers of this clematis are produced in succession from late spring into early summer, with a second flush later in the year, in autumn. The striking, wavy-edged purple petals each have a broad, reddish-mauve stripe down the centre. Pruning group 2 (*see* page 83).

Clematis flammula
Fragrant virgin's bower
○ ◐ ◌ ‖ ❖LATE SUMMER, AUTUMN
H 6m (20ft) S 1m (40in)

This semi-evergreen clematis produces masses of vanilla-scented, snow-white, starry, late-summer flowers. In autumn these are followed by attractive, silky-grey seedheads. It is ideal for growing through an established tree or shrub, or you could allow it to scramble across the soil and make an unusual ground-cover plant in sun or dappled shade. Pruning group 3 (*see* page 84).

Clematis florida 'Pistachio'
○ ‖ ❖LATE SPRING to SUMMER
H 2.5m (8ft) S 3m (10ft)

The alluring, ivory-white flowers that gracefully age to an attractive pale green have rosy-red anthers as a finishing flourish. It flowers for a long period from late spring into summer, against mid-green foliage. Try it alongside the patio or perhaps as a partner to a wall-trained, evergreen California lilac (*Ceanothus*). Pruning group 2 (*see* page 83).

Clematis florida var. sieboldiana
○ ‖ ❖LATE SPRING to SUMMER
H 2m (6ft) S 1m (40in)

This terrific, compact, mid-season clematis with single, white flowers is unusual because the blooms are dominated by an extravagant spiky boss of deep-purple stamens. It flowers for a long period, during late spring and throughout the summer months. You can weave it in an informal fashion through an evergreen hedge in full sun, or train it up a trellis beside the patio. Pruning group 2 (*see* page 83).

Clematis 'General Sikorski'
○ ◐ ⅰⅰ ❖EARLY SUMMER, EARLY AUTUMN
H 3m (10ft) S 1m (40in)

This strong-growing, large-flowered clematis bears large mauve flowers, with overlapping petals and contrasting creamy anthers, against a backdrop of dark foliage. It flowers during early summer and sometimes in early autumn, too. Although fairly vigorous, it makes an excellent container plant, or train it up an arch to show off the numerous beautiful flowers to best effect. Pruning group 2 (*see* opposite).

Clematis 'Gillian Blades'
○ ◐ ⅰⅰ
❖LATE SPRING to EARLY SUMMER, EARLY AUTUMN
H 2.5m (8ft) S 1m (40in)

A charming clematis, this will add a touch of sophistication to a well-established shrub or tree with its elegant 15cm (6in) wide, pinkish-white flowers that gradually fade to pure white. The overlapping, wavy-edged petals have a central eye of creamy anthers. It flowers in late spring and again in early autumn. Pruning group 2 (*see* opposite).

Clematis 'Gipsy Queen'
○ ◑ ⅰⅰ ❖MIDSUMMER to EARLY AUTUMN
H 3m (10ft) S 1.5m (5ft)

The paddle-shaped, velvety-purple petals of this clematis, which overlap at their widest point, look like paper cut-outs because they taper to leave gaps around the central boss of stamens. The flowers are carried from midsummer to early autumn. This clematis looks stunning scrambling through shrubs, as well as trained up an obelisk in the border. Pruning group 3 (*see* page 84).

Clematis 'Gravetye Beauty'
○ ◐ ⅰⅰ ❖LATE SUMMER to EARLY AUTUMN
H and S 3m (10ft)

Startling crimson flowers, reminiscent of small, lily-flowered tulips, are produced in succession throughout late summer and into autumn. Try using this sizzling clematis as part of a planting scheme with hot colours, or let it scramble through a pale-leaved shrub, where its bright flowers will stand out. Pruning group 3 (*see* page 84).

Clematis 'Guernsey Cream'
○ ◐ ⅰⅰ ❖LATE SPRING to SUMMER
H and S 2m (6ft)

Rich and tempting, the generous creamy flowers on this large-flowered clematis are produced from late spring and into early summer, with a second flush at the end of the summer. Each bloom has a creamy-yellow central eye. It's worth giving this climber a prominent spot in a pot on the patio, or grow it against a dark backdrop for dramatic emphasis. Pruning group 2 (*see* opposite).

Clematis 'Hagley Hybrid'
◐ ⅰⅰ ❖MIDSUMMER to EARLY AUTUMN
H 2.5m (8ft) S 1m (40in)

Sugar-pink to pinkish-mauve tapering petals, with a central boss of red anthers, give this vigorous yet compact, large-flowered clematis real star quality. It flowers continuously from midsummer to early autumn. Prone to fading in full sun, it is best planted against an east- or west-facing wall or fence and can cope with near-continuous shade, although flowering will be less impressive. Pruning group 3 (*see* page 84).

Clematis 'Happy Anniversary'

○ ◑ ⚏ ❖LATE SPRING, EARLY SUMMER

H 2.5m (8ft) **S** 1m (40in)

The perfect gift for a late-spring or early-summer celebration, this climber will return year after year to reward you with exquisite, dark lavender-blue flowers, each with a spiky, cream and red central boss. Grow it against a wall or fence, train it up an arch, or use it to add height to a border by letting it climb up a wooden or metal obelisk. Pruning group 2 (*see* right).

Clematis 'Huldine'

○ ◑ ⚏ ❖MIDSUMMER to EARLY AUTUMN

H 3m (10ft) **S** 2m (6ft)

A vigorous, late-flowering clematis, this climber is almost smothered in elegant, yellow-eyed, ivory-white, bowl-shaped flowers that are pale mauve underneath. It flowers continuously from midsummer until early autumn. Let it romp over a pergola or fence at the back of a border in sun or partial shade. Pruning group 3 (*see* page 84).

Mid-season clematis: pruning group 2

Flowering in late spring and early summer, plants in this second group produce flowers on old wood, or in other words, on the previous year's shoots. Many of them may also produce a second flush of flowers on the tips of new shoots in late summer.

How and when to prune

Prune clematis in this group in early spring, before new growth begins. Cut out any damaged wood and then prune back the old stems to a strong pair of buds: these will bear flowers in the current season. (*See also* page 59.)

MID-SEASON VARIETIES

Clematis 'Arctic Queen'
C. 'Barbara Jackman'
C. 'Bees' Jubilee'
C. 'Blue Eyes'
C. 'Crystal Fountain'
C. 'Doctor Ruppel'
C. 'Duchess of Edinburgh'
C. 'Elizabeth'
C. 'Fireworks'
C. 'Fragrant Spring'
C. 'Freda'
C. 'General Sikorski'
C. 'Gillian Blades'
C. 'Guernsey Cream'

C. 'Happy Anniversary'
C. 'Lasurstern'
C. 'Marjorie'
C. 'Miss Bateman'
C. 'Niobe'
C. *montana* var. *grandiflora*
C. *montana* var. *rubens* 'Pink Perfection'
C. *montana* var. *rubens* 'Tetrarose'
C. 'Mrs Cholmondeley'
C. 'Multi Blue'
C. 'Nelly Moser'
C. 'The President'
C. 'Vyvyan Pennell'

Clematis 'The President' is growing up and along a dry stone wall, its rich purple blooms echoed by *Verbena bonariensis*.

Clematis 'Jackmanii Superba'

○ ⇊ ❖MIDSUMMER to LATE SUMMER

H 3m (10ft) S 1m (40in)

Opulent, velvety flowers in the deepest and richest shade of purple are beautifully set off by a contrasting spiky boss of stamens. Deservedly popular, this reliable late-flowering clematis blooms throughout mid- and late summer and is a super choice for a prominent trellis, wall or fence. It also looks pretty spectacular trained over an arch. Pruning group 3 (*see* right).

Clematis 'Lasurstern'

○ ◗ ⇊

❖LATE SPRING to EARLY SUMMER

H 2.5m (8ft) S 1m (40in)

A vigorous, large-flowered clematis, it bears blooms of a soothing blue shade, with wavy-edged, overlapping petals radiating from a contrasting creamy-yellow boss of anthers. It produces its 15cm (6in) wide blooms in succession, from late spring into early summer. Grow it against a wall or fence, or up an arch, or cover an obelisk in the border. Pruning group 3 (*see* right).

Late-flowering clematis: pruning group 3

The third group of clematis is mostly made up of large-flowered hybrids that flower in late summer to autumn, but also includes some with smaller blooms. These clematis produce flowers on current season's growth.

How and when to prune

In early spring prune these hard by cutting back all the stems to a pair of strong, healthy buds. The shortened stems should be about 30cm (12in) in height. (*See also* page 59.)

LATE-FLOWERING VARIETIES

C. 'Abundance'
C. 'Alba Luxurians'
C. 'Arabella'
C. x *aromatica*
C. 'Betty Corning'
C. 'Bill MacKenzie'
C. 'Black Prince'
C. 'Cassis'
C. 'Comtesse de Bouchaud'
C. 'Confetti'
C. 'Duchess of Albany'
C. x *durandii*
C. 'Ernest Markham'
C. 'Etoile Violette'
C. *flammula*
C. *florida* var. *flore-pleno*
C. *florida* 'Pistachio'
C. *florida* var. *sieboldiana*
C. 'Fond Memories'
C. 'Gipsy Queen'

C. 'Gravetye Beauty'
C. 'Hagley Hybrid'
C. *henryi*
C. 'Huldine'
C. 'Inspiration'
C. 'Jackmanii Superba'
C. 'Joséphine'
C. 'Madame Julia Correvon'
C. 'Niobe'
C. 'Perle d'Azur'
C. 'Polish Spirit'
C. 'Prince Charles'
C. 'Princess Diana'
C. *rehderiana*
C. 'Romantika'
C. 'Rouge Cardinal'
C. 'Royal Velours'
C. *tangutica*
C. x *triternata* 'Rubromarginata'
C. 'Ville de Lyon'

Clematis 'Perle d'Azur' and a white climbing rose make a cool, classic combination.

Clematis macropetala
○ ◑ ⚏ ❖ LATE SPRING, SUMMER

H 2m (6ft) S 1.5m (5ft)

Beautiful, bell-shaped, violet-blue flowers with creamy centres decorate this early-flowering clematis. Attractive, silky seedheads follow on after and provide additional interest throughout summer. It is a good choice for all but north-facing sites, which won't offer shelter from cold winds. Good varieties: 'Lagoon' (deep-blue flowers, shown above); 'Jan Lindmark' (mauve flowers). Pruning group 1 (*see* page 78).

Clematis 'Madame Julia Correvon'
○ ⚏ ❖ MIDSUMMER to LATE AUTUMN

H 3m (10ft) S 1.5m (5ft)

Masses of wine-red, bell-shaped flowers with twisted petals transform this late-flowering clematis from midsummer through to late autumn. The central spiky boss is made up of yellow anthers. Compact and free-flowering, it makes an excellent container plant. Pruning group 3 (*see* opposite).

Clematis 'Marie Boisselot'
○ ◑ ⚏ ❖ EARLY SUMMER to EARLY AUTUMN

H 3m (10ft) S 1m (40in)

Plate-sized flowers that look as if they are made from white satin feature overlapping petals and a spidery central boss of creamy anthers. They are produced in succession from early summer through to early autumn. Grow this clematis against a wall or fence or up an arch, where the large, exquisite flowers can be viewed at close quarters. Pruning group 2 (*see* page 83).

Clematis 'Marjorie'
○ ◑ ⚏ ❖ LATE SPRING to SUMMER

H 10m (33ft) S 3m (10ft)

Cover a pergola or several fence panels with this vigorous, early-flowering clematis. Its bronze-tinged foliage bears striking, cross-shaped, icing-sugar pink flowers with ivory centres, during late spring and early summer. The delicate blooms are followed by silky seedheads that extend its season of interest. Pruning group 1 (*see* page 78).

Clematis 'Markham's Pink'
○ ◑ ⚏ ❖ SPRING, SUMMER

H 10m (33ft) S 3m (10ft)

Beautiful, bell-shaped, candyfloss-pink flowers with creamy centres decorate this early-flowering clematis. Attractive, silky seedheads follow the delicate flowers and provide interest throughout the summer. It is the perfect clematis for training over an arch or covering a fence in a prominent position. Pruning group 1 (*see* page 78).

Clematis 'Miss Bateman'
○ ◑ ⚏ ❖ EARLY SUMMER, LATE SUMMER to AUTUMN

H 2.5m (8ft) S 1m (40in)

Rounded, single, white, early-summer flowers with overlapping petals are striped green when they first open. Each flower has a striking central boss of red anthers. A second flush follows between late summer and early autumn. Grow it against a wall or fence or up an arch, where the attractive flowers can be seen up close. This is a compact clematis and so is a good choice for containers. Pruning group 2 (*see* page 83).

Clematis montana var. rubens
○ ◐ ◔ ⬍ ❖LATE SPRING to EARLY SUMMER
H 10m (33ft) S 3m (10ft)

Vigorous, floriferous and one of the early-flowering varieties, this clematis has purple-flushed foliage and bears masses of pink flowers with creamy centres throughout late spring and early summer. This is a romping clematis and needs plenty of space, so in most gardens you would be better off growing one of the less vigorous, close relatives. Good varieties: 'Pink Perfection' (scented pink flowers); 'Tetrarose' (satiny pink flowers, shown above). Pruning group 1 (*see* page 78).

Clematis 'Mrs Cholmondeley'
○ ◐ ⬍
❖LATE SPRING to EARLY SUMMER, EARLY AUTUMN
H 2m (6ft) S 1m (40in)

Delicate-looking, large, lavender-blue flowers are borne on this clematis from late spring into early summer, with a second flush during early autumn. Grow it against a wall or fence or up an arch, where the blooms can be seen up close. Pruning group 2 (*see* page 83).

Clematis 'Multi Blue'
○ ◐ ⬍ ❖LATE SPRING to EARLY SUMMER, EARLY AUTUMN
H 4m (13ft) S 2m (6ft)

The large, rosette-like, double, deep-blue flowers of this climber have a matching frill of pale blue in the centre. An eye-catching variety, it looks a picture from late spring and into early summer, with a second flush later in the year. Grow it up a pergola or over an arch in sun or partial shade. Pruning group 1 (*see* page 78).

Clematis napaulensis
○ ⬍ ❖WINTER
H 4m (13ft) S 3m (10ft)

This unusual, vigorous, winter-flowering clematis looks lifeless for most of the summer, then in autumn it suddenly gets its act together and produces fresh foliage followed by a crop of fragrant, greenish-yellow, bell-shaped flowers with purple anthers. It can be a real talking point for a spot close to a path or doorway and needs no pruning.

Clematis 'Nelly Moser'
○ ◐ ⬍
❖LATE SPRING to EARLY SUMMER, EARLY AUTUMN
H 3m (10ft) S 1m (40in)

Love it or hate it, 'Nelly Moser' is one of the most recognizable varieties of clematis because of its distinctive candy-striped flowers. Each bloom is pinkish mauve, with a striking, deep-pink central banding to each petal. The flowers are borne from late spring into early summer, with a second flush in early autumn. Grow it up a pergola or arch. Pruning group 2 (*see* page 83).

Clematis 'Niobe'
○ ◐ ⬍ ❖SUMMER to EARLY AUTUMN
H 2m (6ft) S 1m (40in)

At the top of many garden designers' lists of clematis, this heart-warming, ruby-red beauty bears its single, 15cm (6in) wide flowers throughout summer into early autumn. Each bloom has a golden eye of spidery anthers. Compact and easy to grow, it is ideal for pots and looks particularly good in dappled shade, where its deep-red flowers help create a brooding atmosphere. Pruning group 2 (*see* page 83).

Clematis 'Perle d'Azur'

○ ◐ ‡‡ ❖ LATE SUMMER to EARLY AUTUMN

H 3m (10ft) S 1m (40in)

This beautiful and vigorous, blue-flowered variety bears open, yellow-eyed, sky-blue flowers that curl at the tips, throughout late summer to early autumn. Compact and free-flowering, it makes an excellent container climber or a good companion for a climbing rose on an arch or a pergola. Pruning group 3 (*see* page 84).

Clematis 'Prince Charles'

○ ◐ ‡‡ ❖ LATE SUMMER to EARLY AUTUMN

H 2.5m (8ft) S 1.5m (5ft)

Attractive and free-flowering, this large-flowered clematis bears masses of delicate, mauve-blue blooms from late summer until early autumn. An easy-to-grow variety that is fairly compact, it's ideal for small gardens. Pruning group 3 (*see* page 84).

Clematis rehderiana

○ ◐ ‡‡ ❖ SUMMER to AUTUMN

H 6m (20ft) S 2m (6ft)

This very unusual, attractive clematis bears clusters of tiny, bell-shaped, pale yellow flowers, with a refreshing fragrance throughout summer and into autumn. This vigorous and late-flowering climber will light up a wall or fence where it catches the sun. Pruning group 3 (*see* page 84).

Clematis 'Polish Spirit'

○ ◐ ‡‡ ❖ LATE SUMMER to EARLY AUTUMN

H 5m (16ft) S 2m (6ft)

This easy-to-grow variety produces trendy, rich purple blooms that are borne in profusion throughout late summer and into early autumn. The small, saucer-shaped flowers are about 5cm (2in) wide and have anthers that seem to be perfecty matched in colour. Grow it on walls and fences or up arches and pergolas, in sun or dappled shade. Pruning group 3 (*see* page 84).

Clematis 'Princess Diana'

○ ◐ ‡‡ ❖ LATE SUMMER to EARLY AUTUMN

H 2.5m (8ft) S 1m (40in)

Startling, flamingo-pink, tulip-shaped flowers are produced during late summer and into early autumn, against a curtain of fresh green leaves. Grow it on walls and fences, or up arches and pergolas, in sun or dappled shade. This eye-catching, late-flowering clematis is ideal for giving your garden a colour boost when other plants are on the wane. Pruning group 3 (*see* page 84).

Clematis 'Romantika'

○ ◐ ‡‡ ❖ LATE SUMMER

H 2.5m (8ft) S 2m (6ft)

Rich, velvety, dark violet-purple flowers, each with a contrasting yellow eye, are produced in profusion on this lovely late summer flowering clematis. Each bloom is up to 15cm (6in) across. It is a good choice for covering a garden wall or fence that receives some direct sunlight. Pruning group 3 (*see* page 84).

Clematis 'Rouge Cardinal'
○ ↕↕ ❖SUMMER
H 6m (20ft) S 2m (6ft)

The sumptuous, red-velvet, midsummer flowers, with colour-coordinated reddish-purple centres, stand out against a backdrop of fresh green leaves. Each bloom is about 10cm (4in) across. A stunning compact variety, it can be grown over an arch or a trellis, or perhaps left to scramble through a well-established climbing rose in full sun. Pruning group 3 (*see* page 84).

Clematis tangutica
○ ◐ ↕↕ ❖LATE SUMMER, AUTUMN
H 5m (16ft) S 2m (6ft)

Light up partially shaded walls and fences with the cheerful, yellow, late-summer lanterns on this vigorous clematis. The flowers are freely produced and then followed by deliciously fluffy seedheads (shown above). This clematis is a good choice for pergolas and arches. Pruning group 3 (*see* page 84).

Clematis × triternata 'Rubromarginata'
○ ◐ ↕↕ ❖LATE SUMMER
H 4m (13ft) S 2m (6ft)

A lovely, vigorous, old-fashioned clematis, this variety bears masses of fragrant, magenta-edged purple flowers that fade gracefully with age. It is ideal for covering a garden fence, or train it on an arch over a seat where you can appreciate its unusual fragrance. Pruning group 3 (*see* page 84).

Clematis 'Royal Velours'
○ ↕↕ ❖SUMMER to AUTUMN
H 3m (10ft) S 1.5m (5ft)

Striking, red-purple, velvety flowers, each with a creamy eye and red stamens, are produced in abundance against a curtain of fresh green leaves. This easy-to-grow climber is said to be resistant to clematis wilt disease and is pretty good at surviving wind and heavy rain, too. It is a great choice for scrambling over an arch or trellis and prefers full sun. Pruning group 3 (*see* page 84).

Clematis 'The President'
○ ↕↕ ❖EARLY to MIDSUMMER
H 2m (6ft) S 1m (40in)

The regal, rich-purple flowers of this clematis are up to 15cm (6in) wide, with slightly wavy, pointed petals that are silvery underneath. A crop of red anthers adorns the centre. Blooming from early to midsummer, it really puts on a show. Compact and easy to grow, this is an ideal clematis for planting in a patio container in full sun. Pruning group 2 (*see* page 83).

Clematis 'Ville de Lyon'
○ ◐ ↕↕ ❖LATE SUMMER to EARLY AUTUMN
H 2m (6ft) S 1m (40in)

Carmine-red flowers that darken towards the edge are each set off by a contrasting centre of golden anthers. Blooming freely and continuously in late summer and into autumn, this clematis offers great garden value. You can grow it on walls and fences, or up arches and pergolas, in sun or dappled shade. Pruning group 3 (*see* page 84).

Clematis 'Vyvyan Pennell'

○ ◐ ‖
❖LATE SPRING to EARLY SUMMER, EARLY AUTUMN

H 3m (10ft) S 1m (40in)

This dramatic, double, large-flowered clematis produces blowsy, multi-layered blooms in shades of purple, mauve and violet, set off by a golden crop of anthers in the centre. The flowers are borne from late spring into early summer, with a second flush in early autumn. It is an excellent climber for softening the edges of an arch or pergola in sun or dappled shade. Pruning group 2 (*see* page 83).

Clematis 'Willy' Alpine clematis

○ ◐ ‖ ❖EARLY SPRING, AUTUMN

H 2m (6ft) S 1.5m (5ft)

This pretty, early-flowering climber bears delicate, nodding, bell-shaped, pale pink blooms, which are a deeper shade at the base, with contrasting creamy anthers. The flowers appear in early spring and are followed by fluffy seedheads in early autumn. It is ideal for all but north-facing walls and fences. Pruning group 1 (*see* page 78).

Cobaea scandens
Cup-and-saucer vine

○ ✺ ‖ ❖MIDSUMMER to EARLY AUTUMN

H 10m (33ft) S 3m (10ft)

Exotic-looking, bell-shaped flowers adorn this evergreen, perennial climber from midsummer. Usually grown as an annual, it adds interest to the base of an established climber and can be trained up a sheltered, sunny trellis. This is a useful climber for a conservatory. Good variety: f. 'Alba' (white; shown above).

Coronilla valentina subsp. glauca 'Citrina'

○ ❄ ‖ ❖LATE WINTER to EARLY SPRING

H and S 80cm (32in)

A dense, bushy evergreen with blue-green foliage, this shrub bears attractive, fragrant, lemon-yellow, pea-like flowers from late winter until early spring. A borderline-hardy plant, it needs the protection of a warm, sunny wall or fence to survive the winter.

Cotoneaster horizontalis

○ ◐ ● ‖ ❖EARLY SUMMER, AUTUMN

H 1m (40in) S 1.5m (5ft)

This reliable wall shrub produces an attractive herringbone pattern of branches. It is encrusted with tiny, pinkish-white, early-summer flowers, followed by scarlet, autumn berries that are loved by birds. The tiny, glossy, dark green leaves look neat all summer and take on lovely autumn hues. A good choice for a north-facing wall, it will grow happily in most situations.

Cytisus battandieri
Pineapple broom

○ ◌ ‖ pH→ −pH ❖MID- to LATE SUMMER

H and S 5m (16ft)

This gorgeous, tree-like shrub has attractive, silver-grey, laburnum-like foliage, providing the perfect backdrop for its exotic-looking, lemon-yellow spikes of deliciously pineapple-scented flowers in mid- to late summer. Train it against a sunny wall to show off its flowers and to give it the protection and dry soil it prefers.

Dregea sinensis
○ ◑ ❄ ⬇⬇ ❖SUMMER

H 3m (10ft) S 2m (6ft)

Clusters of fragrant, creamy-coloured flowers, spotted with pink or red inside, are the main attraction of this evergreen twining climber. Its heart-shaped leaves look good throughout the year. You may need to tie new growth into the support until the plant starts to climb naturally.

Eccremocarpus scaber
Chilean glory flower
○ ❄ ⬇⬇ 🍂 ❖SUMMER

H and S 3m (10ft)

This fast-growing, evergreen, perennial climber is usually grown as an annual. It will produce exotic-looking, loose spikes of orange-red, tubular flowers all summer long if given the shelter of a sunny wall or fence. After the last frost, plant it out at the foot of its support in soil that's been enriched with well-rotted organic matter.

Euonymus fortunei
○ ◑ ● ⬇⬇ ❖YEAR-ROUND

H 60cm (2ft) S indefinite

A reliable garden stalwart, this evergreen shrub has dark green, leathery leaves. Variegated forms are excellent for brightening up shady borders. Inconspicuous clusters of tiny, green, early-summer flowers are followed by spherical white fruits. This is an ideal understorey plant that can be grown in shade in a shrub border or trained against a wall. Good variety: 'Emerald 'n' Gold' (bright yellow-edged leaves that are pink-tinged in winter; shown above).

Fallopia baldschuanica
Mile-a-minute, Russian vine
○ ◑ ⬇⬇ ❖LATE SUMMER

H 12m (39ft) S 4m (13ft)

A brute of a climber, the Russian vine can cover large outbuildings or garden structures in just a few seasons. During late summer it's smothered with sprays of tiny, funnel-shaped, pink-flushed white flowers. Use this plant with care, since it may soon outgrow its allotted space and can be overwhelming.

Fremontodendron
'California Glory' Flannel bush
○ ❄ ⬇⬇ pH➡ –pH↑ ❖SUMMER

H 6m (20ft) S 4m (13ft)

Rich buttercup-yellow, waxy-looking, cup-shaped flowers are produced in succession throughout the summer on this shrub, which has handsome, fig-like, evergreen foliage. It will soak up the sun to produce a radiant glow on a south-facing wall or fence. Contact with the foliage can sometimes cause skin irritation; as a precaution, plant it at the back of a border.

Garrya elliptica 'James Roof'
Silk-tassel bush
○ ◑ ● ⬇⬇ ❖WINTER

H and S 4m (13ft)

Utilitarian and pollution-tolerant, this evergreen wall shrub is ideal for covering urban walls and fences with a cloak of wavy-edged, green foliage. In winter it is lit up by elegant, silvery, tassel-like male catkins. It makes an attractive foil for other plants during the growing season. Another good variety: 'Glasnevin Wine' (purple-stained catkins).

Hedera algeriensis
North African ivy

○ ◐ ● ❄ ↕↕ pH→ −pH↑ ❖YEAR-ROUND

H 4m (13ft) S 5m (16ft)

Huge, shining, yellow-evergreen leaves, with creamy edges and on dark red stalks, provide a cloak of foliage over vertical surfaces. This ivy is perfect for brightening up partially shaded corners that are sheltered from cold winds; it is also good for containers on a sheltered patio. Good variety: 'Gloire de Marengo' (silvery leaves; shown above).

Hedera colchica Persian ivy

○ ◐ ● ↕↕ pH→ −pH↑ ❖YEAR-ROUND

H 10m (33ft) S 5m (16ft)

This handsome, vigorous, evergreen climber has large, shiny, heart-shaped, dark green leaves. It is ideal for covering dry, shady areas under shrubs and trees and will quickly smother walls and fences, but will need regular cutting back to keep within bounds. Variegated forms will also help brighten up gloomy corners and passageways. Good variety: 'Dentata Variegata' (light green leaves with paler edges; shown above).

Hedera helix Common ivy

○ ◐ ● pH→ −pH↑ 🍂 ❖YEAR-ROUND

H 10m (33ft) S 5m (16ft)

Most people are familiar with the glossy, dark green leaves of this ivy. A vigorous, self-clinging, evergreen climber, once mature it will produce sprays of yellowish-green autumn flowers, followed by spherical, black fruits. It is a first choice for covering dry, shady areas under trees and shrubs, and will quickly cover walls and fences. Cut back regularly to keep it within bounds. Good variety: 'Goldchild' (yellow-edged leaves; shown above).

Holboellia coriacea

○ ◐ ● ❄ ↕↕ 🍂 ❖SPRING, SUMMER

H 7m (23ft) S 3m (10ft)

An unusual and interesting twining evergreen, this climber has attractive, divided foliage with large, loose clusters of dangling, bell-shaped, purplish-pink spring flowers that are sometimes followed by sausage-shaped fruits. It needs protection from cold winds, so a sheltered wall is an ideal site.

Humulus lupulus 'Aureus'
Golden hop

○ ◐ ● ↕↕ ❖SPRING, SUMMER

H and S 6m (20ft)

The handsome, deeply lobed, vine-like yellow-green leaves of this herbaceous climber quickly cover arches, trellis and fences in sun or dappled shade. In summer, female plants bear yellowish-green, hop-like flower spikes. Tie in the early growth to get it started. It is ideal for informal settings and as a backdrop to cottage-style planting schemes.

Hydrangea anomala subsp. petiolaris Climbing hydrangea

○ ◐ ● ◆ ↕↕ ❖LATE SPRING to EARLY SUMMER

H 15m (49ft) S 3m (10ft)

Light up dark walls in spring and summer with this useful and vigorous, self-clinging climber. The delicate, creamy-white, lacecap flowers that appear in late spring and early summer stand out against the backdrop of dark green leaves, which turn butter yellow in autumn. Bear in mind that this climber is deciduous, although the woody stems provide some interest in winter.

Ipomoea purpurea 'Heavenly Blue' Morning glory

◯ ❄ ↓↓ ❖LATE SUMMER

H and **S** 2m (6ft)

From late summer onwards, a succession of white-throated, sky-blue trumpets, up to 6cm (2½in) across, open each morning and last just one day on this lovely annual climber. Use it to provide instant colour on any vertical surface in full sun. Feed and water the plant regularly for a flush of blooms every day.

Itea ilicifolia

◯ ❄ ↓↓ ❖LATE SUMMER

H and **S** 3m (10ft)

A real talking point, this understated, fountain-shaped, evergreen shrub is worth considering if you have the space. With dark green, holly-like foliage, its huge, cascading 45cm (18in) long cat's tails of fragrant, tiny, greenish-white flowers are the undoubted highlight during late summer. Plant it in a sheltered spot, such as against a south-facing wall or fence, where it will be protected from cold winter winds.

Jasminum beesianum

◯ ◐ ❄ ↓↓ ❖EARLY SUMMER

H and **S** 5m (16ft)

This slightly fragrant, evergreen or semi-evergreen, pink-flowering jasmine blooms in early summer on twining stems. Not as vigorous as common jasmine, it is an ideal choice for adding colour to a trellis in the conservatory or a sheltered spot in sun or partial shade.

Jasminum nudiflorum

Winter jasmine

◯ ◐ ● ↓↓ ❖WINTER

H and **S** 3m (10ft)

Uplifting, sunny-yellow, tubular flowers appear on the bare, arching, green stems of this shrub from midwinter onwards, really brightening up dingy days when little else is in bloom. Very easy to grow and reliable, it can be left to form an informal clump or be trained against a wall or fence.

Jasminum officinale

Common jasmine

◯ ◐ ❄ ↓↓ ❖MIDSUMMER to AUTUMN

H 12m (39ft) **S** 3m (10ft)

Understandably popular, this climber carries clusters of sweetly scented, white flowers from midsummer until autumn. An excellent choice for a sheltered wall or fence, this jasmine is also perfect for growing over trellis and an arch next to a seating area. Good varieties: 'Argenteovariegatum' (variegated leaves); 'Fiona Sunrise' (yellow leaves).

Jasminum officinale 'Devon Cream' (syn. 'Clotted Cream')

◯ ◐ ❄ ↓↓ ❖SUMMER

H and **S** 3m (10ft)

A sweetly scented jasmine, this bears large flowers of a rich cream colour in succession from early to late summer. Fast-growing and free-flowering, it's ideal for covering an ugly wall or fence in a sheltered spot, but to really make the most of its fragrance, plant it near a much-used path or over an arch by the garden or house entrance.

Jasminum × *stephanense*
○ ◐ ❄ ↧↥ ❖EARLY SUMMER

H and S 5m (16ft)

This twining climber has pale pink, fragrant flowers and pretty foliage that is intricately cream-edged when young; as a result, this jasmine is ornamental even when it isn't flowering. It is useful for covering vertical surfaces and garden structures in sheltered spots in sun or partial shade. Plant it where the scent lingers, especially next to a gate, an entrance or a path.

Lathyrus odoratus Sweet pea
○ ◐ ↧↥ 🍃 ❖LATE SUMMER

H and S 2m (6ft)

Every garden should have space for a handful of these classic, sweetly fragrant, annual flowers, which come in a range of colours, which include shades of red, purple, rose, lilac and white. Grow them up a trellis or an obelisk in a sunny border or in a large pot up a wigwam of strings. Plant a few and you'll get a continuous supply of flowers for cutting.

Lonicera × *brownii* 'Dropmore Scarlet' Scarlet trumpet honeysuckle
○ ◐ ◖ ↧↥ 🍃 ❖LATE SUMMER

H 4m (13ft) S 2m (6ft)

This compact honeysuckle, with bluish-green, sometimes semi-evergreen foliage, will add charm to an obelisk or garden divider. The stunning, flaming-scarlet, tubular, late-summer flowers are followed in warm summers by red berries. Although not fragrant, it still makes a lovely garden plant.

Lathyrus latifolius Everlasting pea
○ ◐ ↧↥ 🍃 ❖SUMMER to EARLY AUTUMN

H and S 2m (6ft)

This perennial sweet pea bears a succession of pinkish-purple blooms from summer onwards. It is a great little herbaceous climber, best suited to cottage-garden schemes in full sun or partial shade, where it will cover trellis, the side of an arch, or the post of a pergola. It is an easy alternative to annual sweet peas. Good variety: 'White Pearl' (white flowers; shown above).

Lonicera × *americana*
Honeysuckle
○ ◐ ◖ ↧↥ 🍃 ❖SUMMER

H 7m (23ft) S 2m (6ft)

A vigorous climber, this honeysuckle produces a succession of pinky-purple buds that open to reveal highly fragrant, purple-flushed, yellow, tubular blooms throughout the summer. Bright red berries sometimes follow in good summers. Grown over a pergola or arch, or used as a backdrop on a wall or fence, it is an excellent choice for a cottage-style garden scheme.

Lonicera henryi Honeysuckle
○ ◐ ❄ ◖ ↧↥ 🍃 ❖EARLY SUMMER

H 10m (33ft) S 1m (40in)

Gorgeous, purple-red, tubular flowers with contrasting yellow throats are produced in whorls during early summer. Small, purple-black fruits follow. This is a charming choice for a prominent screen, where its evergreen foliage will provide year-round cover. It also makes a good backdrop to a cottage-style garden border.

Lonicera japonica 'Halliana'
Japanese honeysuckle

○ ◑ ◍ ‼ 🍃 ❖MID-SPRING to LATE SUMMER

H 10m (33ft) S 2m (6ft)

This vigorous and very fragrant evergreen honeysuckle bears a succession of white, tubular flowers that gradually change to yellow from mid-spring until late summer. With a long flowering period and attractive foliage, it is ideal for an arch or pergola in a prominent position. In warm summers, purple-black fruits follow the flowers.

Lonicera periclymenum
Common honeysuckle, Woodbine

○ ◑ ◍ ‼ 🍃 ❖LATE SPRING to SUMMER

H 7m (23ft) S 1m (40in)

Deliciously honey-scented, tubular, purple-budded flowers that open to reveal a buff-yellow throat are produced in succession from late spring. This early honeysuckle is a great choice for covering a wall or fence in full sun or partial shade and will release its fragrance in the evening. Good variety: 'Serotina' (shown above).

Magnolia grandiflora

○ ◑ ‼ 🍃 🍂 ❖LATE SUMMER

H 6m (20ft) S 15m (49ft)

This is perhaps one of the only trees that looks better trained against a wall. It needs a very large wall, but in time will reward you with huge, fragrant, snow-white, bowl-shaped flowers, which emerge from furry buds right at the end of the summer. The evergreen leaves are impressive too: large and leathery, they are glossy, dark green above with rusty hairs underneath.

Lonicera japonica var. repens
Japanese honeysuckle

○ ◑ ◍ ‼ 🍃 ❖MID-SPRING to LATE SUMMER

H 10m (33ft) S 3m (10ft)

This long-flowering, twining evergreen is perfect for covering an arch, pergola or garden building with highly fragrant, tubular, white flowers that become yellow as they age. The charming flowers are often purple-flushed and borne in succession from mid-spring until late summer. Small, purple-black fruits follow, making this a great choice for an informal wildlife garden.

Lonicera × tellmanniana
Honeysuckle

○ ◑ ◍ ‼ 🍃 ❖LATE SPRING to EARLY SUMMER

H 5m (16ft) S 1.2m (4ft)

Splendid and unusually coloured, this honeysuckle produces a succession of red-flushed buds that open in late spring and early summer to reveal striking coppery-orange, tubular blooms. Although not fragrant, it is worth growing for its stunning flowers, which would form a perfect backdrop to a fiery planting combination of reds, yellows and oranges.

Parthenocissus henryana
Chinese Virginia creeper

○ ◑ ❄ ‼ ❖AUTUMN

H 10m (33ft) S 5m (16ft)

This beautiful climber has strokeable, velvety, dark green leaves decorated with white and pink veins. The foliage turns fiery shades of scarlet in autumn. Virginia creepers are an ideal choice for covering south-, east- or west-facing walls and fences; they colour best in partial shade. Chinese Virginia creeper is less vigorous than other *Parthenocissus* species and ideal for smaller gardens.

Parthenocissus quinquefolia
Virginia creeper
○ ◐ ● ❉ ↓↓ ❖AUTUMN

H 15m (49ft) S 5m (16ft)

Perhaps the best ornamental creeper for autumn colour, this climber has attractive, deeply divided leaves that ignite into dramatic, fiery shades of crimson before they fall to the ground. This vigorous Virginia creeper is ideal for covering large expanses of east-, west- or north-facing walls or fences, as long as they aren't too cold in winter.

Parthenocissus tricuspidata
Boston ivy
○ ◐ ● ❉ ↓↓ ❖AUTUMN

H 20m (65ft) S 10m (33ft)

This vigorous, handsome, ornamental creeper is particularly noted for its spectacular colour in autumn, when its large, deeply lobed, dark green leaves turn dramatic shades of blood red and purple. It can be used to cover north-, east- or west-facing walls and fences that do not get too cold in winter. Good variety: 'Veitchii' (good autumn tints; shown above).

Passiflora caerulea
Blue passion flower
○ ◐ ◐ ↓↓ ❖SUMMER

H 10m (33ft) S 2m (6ft)

Exotic blue and white, fragrant passion flowers, up to 10cm (4in) across, are borne in summer, followed in warm summers by egg-shaped, yellow fruits. It is fast-growing with rich evergreen leaves. Grow this climber at the back of a tropical-themed border or up a sunny pergola or screen next to the patio, where the intricate flowers can be seen at close quarters.

Pileostegia viburnoides
○ ◐ ● ❉ ↓↓ ❖LATE SUMMER

H 6m (20ft) S 2m (6ft)

This lovely evergreen with handsome, glossy, leathery leaves produces frothy clusters, up to 15cm (6in) wide, of starry, cream-coloured flowers during late summer. It is worth considering for a very sheltered fence or wall, or even for scrambling through an established tree. Slow-growing, it can take time to establish before flowering.

Piptanthus nepalensis
Evergreen laburnum
○ ◐ ❉ ↓↓ ❖SPRING to SUMMER, AUTUMN

H 2.5m (8ft) S 2m (6ft)

Despite its common name, this erect-growing shrub is usually less than evergreen but still worth growing for its delightful crops of sunny-yellow, pea-like flowers. These are produced in clusters during late spring and early summer. The handsome, bluish-green foliage and the long, hanging seedpods that follow the flowers make this shrub an interesting backdrop at other times.

Pyracantha 'Mohave' Firethorn
○ ◐ ↓↓ ❖EARLY SUMMER, AUTUMN to WINTER

H 4m (13ft) S 3m (10ft)

This popular firethorn can either be grown as a bushy shrub or trained on wires to form a neat, evergreen cladding to walls and fences. During early summer, it produces pretty sprays of small, white flowers, but it is prized for the fabulous crop of bright red berries that follow, lasting well into winter. The colourful, long-lasting fruits are very popular with birds and are an important winter food source.

Pyracantha 'Orange Glow'
Firethorn
○ ◐ ● ◗ ↕↕ ❖ SPRING, AUTUMN to WINTER
H 3m (10ft) S 4m (13ft)

Grown mainly for its abundant clusters of long-lasting orange berries during autumn and winter, this is a superb wall shrub that is loved by native songbirds. It is upright, spiny-stemmed and evergreen, and produces sprays of small white flowers in spring. You could fan-train it against a shaded, east- or west-facing wall or fence, or grow it as a flowering hedge.

Pyracantha 'Saphyr Orange'
Firethorn
○ ◐ ↕↕ ❖ EARLY SUMMER, AUTUMN to WINTER
H 4m (13ft) S 3m (10ft)

This easy-to-grow, disease-resistant firethorn variety bears pretty sprays of small, white, early-summer flowers. They are followed by a fabulous crop of bright orange berries that stand out against the glossy, dark, evergreen foliage. The colourful, long-lasting fruits are loved by birds, too, providing them with much-needed food in winter.

Pyracantha 'Soleil d'Or' Firethorn
○ ◐ ↕↕ ❖ EARLY SUMMER, AUTUMN to WINTER
H 3m (10ft) S 2.5m (8ft)

This naturally upright shrub is easy to train on wires against vertical surfaces, forming a neat evergreen backdrop. During early summer the spine-covered, red-tinged shoots carry pretty clusters of white flowers, which are followed by huge crops of golden-yellow berries. An important source of food for birds in winter, the berries are also highly attractive and long-lasting.

Rhodochiton atrosanguineus
Purple bell vine
○ ◐ ✳ ◗ ↕↕ ❖ EARLY SUMMER to AUTUMN
H and S 3m (10ft)

This exotic-looking, tender perennial climber has pendent flowers reminiscent of those of a fuchsia. They are produced in succession from early summer to the first frosts, in shades of blood red, purple and rose pink. In frost-prone areas, treat this climber as an annual.

Rosa 'Albéric Barbier'
○ ◐ ◗ ↕↕ 🍃 ❖ EARLY SUMMER, LATE SUMMER
H 5m (16ft) S 3m (10ft)

Virtually evergreen, this vigorous, rambling rose produces uplifting sprays of double, slightly scented, creamy-white, early-summer flowers, often with a repeat performance in late summer. The lovely blooms stand out against the glossy, dark green leaves. It is ideal for covering walls, fences and other garden structures in sun or partial shade.

Rosa 'Albertine'
○ ◐ ◗ ↕↕ 🍃 ❖ EARLY SUMMER
H 5m (16ft) S 4m (13ft)

Exquisite, pale salmon-pink, fragrant, double flowers are held on ruddy stems throughout early summer on this vigorous rambler. They are ideal for cutting. Use this rose to cover a large south-facing wall or grow it up and over a sunny pergola.

Rosa 'Aloha'

○ ◑ ◌ ‖ 🍃 ❖MIDSUMMER to EARLY AUTUMN

H and S 2–2.5m (6–8ft)

Rainproof, sweetly scented, large, double, rose-pink and salmon flowers are borne on strong stems throughout midsummer and into early autumn, against handsome, leathery, dark green leaves. Use this vigorous climbing rose to cover a sunny wall or fence, or train it over a pergola.

Rosa banksiae 'Lutea'

Yellow banksian rose

○ ◑ ◌ ‖ 🍃 ❖SPRING

H and S 6m (20ft)

One of the earliest-flowering roses, this charming rambler bears garlands of small, double, butter-yellow blooms with a subtle fragrance (reminiscent of violets) from mid-spring. It does best on a sheltered wall in full sun, but will also tolerate dappled shade.

Rosa 'Climbing Iceberg'

○ ◑ ◌ ‖ 🍃 ❖LATE SUMMER to AUTUMN

H and S 3m (10ft)

Popular in white planting schemes, this superb, pure white rose bears its double, subtly fragrant blooms in sprays throughout late summer and into autumn. It is repeat-flowering. A sight to behold growing on a sunny wall or fence, this climber will need to be dead-headed regularly to keep it pristine and flowering well.

Rosa 'American Pillar'

○ ◑ ◌ ‖ 🍃 ❖MIDSUMMER

H 5m (16ft) S 4m (13ft)

Vigorous, even rampant, this rambler rose bears huge clusters of single, white-eyed, carmine-red flowers during midsummer. Train the pliable stems over a sturdy pergola or along a fence in sun or partial shade. It can be troubled by disease, particularly mildew, and needs regular pruning to keep it within bounds.

Rosa 'Bantry Bay'

○ ◑ ◌ ‖ 🍃 ❖LATE SUMMER to EARLY AUTUMN

H 4m (13ft) S 2.5m (8ft)

Subtly scented, semi-double, deep rose-pink flowers are borne in clusters during late summer and into early autumn, against dark green leaves. A repeat-flowering climber with a free-branching habit, it's an ideal choice for a pillar or for covering a sunny wall or fence. It has shown good disease and rain resistance.

Rosa 'Compassion'

○ ◑ ◌ ‖ 🍃 ❖LATE SUMMER

H 3m (10ft) S 2.5m (8ft)

Lovely, apricot-flushed, salmon-pink, double flowers are produced in profusion during late summer on this repeat-flowering climbing rose. Grow it up a sunny wall close to a path to really appreciate the other great feature of this variety – its appealing fragrance.

Rosa 'Constance Spry'
○ ◐ ◗ ♦ ‼ ♨ ❖SUMMER
H and S 2–3m (6–10ft)

This stunning, vigorous climbing rose produces deliciously fragrant, double, rose-pink flowers up to 12cm (5in) across on arching stems that are clothed in grey-green foliage. A well-loved English rose, it is a great choice for growing up a post or obelisk in the border, for covering a trellis, or training up a wall or fence panel. It is a vigorous variety that can be kept shrubby by annual pruning.

Rosa 'Emily Gray'
○ ◐ ◗ ♦ ‼ ♨ ❖MIDSUMMER
H 5m (16ft) S 3m (10ft)

The buff-yellow, double flowers of this rambler are produced in fragrant sprays in midsummer against glossy, dark green foliage. The leaves are bronze-tinted when young and often retained all year. Good for screening and clothing eyesores, it's also a useful backdrop for spring- and autumn-flowering plants.

Rosa 'Etoile de Hollande'
○ ◐ ◗ ♦ ‼ ♨ ❖LATE SUMMER to AUTUMN
H 4m (13ft) S 3m (10ft)

This climber has large, sumptuous, velvet-red, double flowers that appear throughout late summer and into autumn. The flowers are strongly scented and will look stunning against a house wall or fence.

Rosa filipes 'Kiftsgate'
○ ◐ ◗ ♦ ‼ ♨ ❖LATE SUMMER to EARLY AUTUMN
H 10m (33ft) S 6m (20ft)

This rapidly growing rambler produces huge sprays of single, fragrant, creamy-coloured flowers throughout late summer and early autumn, followed by glossy red hips. It is a good choice for covering large expanses of wall or fence, clothing buildings and eyesores or adding interest to a mature tree.

Rosa 'Generous Gardener'
○ ◐ ◗ ♦ ‼ ♨ ❖SUMMER
H and S 2.5m (8ft)

A glorious, thornless climbing rose, 'Generous Gardener' produces elegant, arching stems bearing clusters of fragrant, double, pale pink flowers that shine out against lustrous, dark green foliage during the summer. The flowers darken in tone later in the year. It is ideal for covering sheltered, sunny walls and fences, and is also disease-resistant.

Rosa 'Gloire de Dijon'
Old glory rose
○ ◐ ◗ ♦ ‼ ♨ ❖LATE SUMMER to AUTUMN
H 5m (16ft) S 4m (13ft)

Deliciously fragrant, double, buff-yellow flowers are produced during late summer and early autumn, and stand out well against the glossy, dark green foliage. This climber is ideal for training up walls and fences, where the flowers can be enjoyed easily. Mildew can be a problem.

Climbing and rambler roses

Climbers and ramblers aren't as easy to tell apart as you might think, mainly because, in recent times, rose breeders have combined elements of both groups to produce new varieties. True ramblers are related to wild roses and are more vigorous than climbers; they will very quickly outgrow their allotted space. Some points of difference between the two types are outlined below.

Rambler roses

With their long, pliable stems, rambler roses are ideal for training along ropes or over arches and pergolas. They flower only once, for a few weeks in summer, usually around midsummer. The flowers are borne on the growth produced the previous year, so stems that have flowered need to be pruned directly afterwards. Cut them back to the base or to a younger sideshoot that has not flowered (*see* page 58). The new growth then needs to be tied into the support in preparation for flowering next year.

Super-sized ramblers

Some ramblers are so vigorous that 'rampant' might be a better description. If you have limited space in the garden, think twice about planting *Rosa filipes* 'Kiftsgate' or *R.* 'Rambling Rector'.

Climbing roses

Most climbing roses are repeat-flowering so are good value and will provide a much longer display than

Rosa 'Rambling Rector' looks stunning scrambling along a rope swag.

rambler roses. They benefit from regular dead-heading, which will help prolong the display. Pruning isn't essential for climbers, although they will perform and look better if sideshoots are shortened in late autumn or winter and old barren wood is replaced with younger, more productive stems (*see* page 58).

Climbing roses have stiff stems that are more difficult to tie into garden structures such as arches and pergolas than are the stems of ramblers. They are ideal, though, for clothing a post.

The climbers *Rosa* 'New Dawn' and 'Aloha' and *Clematis* 'Ville de Lyon' combine to create a lovely, sweetly scented arbour.

OTHER CLIMBING VARIETIES
Rosa 'Bantry Bay'
R. 'Climbing Iceberg'
R. 'Compassion'
R. 'Constance Spry'
R. 'Danse du Feu'
R. 'Etoile de Hollande'
R. 'Generous Gardener'
R. 'Gloire de Dijon'
R. 'Golden Showers'
R. 'Guinée'
R. 'Handel'
R. 'Madame Alfred Carrière'
R. 'Madame Grégoire Staechelin'
R. 'Maigold'
R. 'Mermaid'
R. 'Mortimer Sackler'
R. 'Paul's Scarlet Climber'
R. 'Schoolgirl'
R. 'A Shropshire Lad'
R. 'Zéphirine Drouhin'

OTHER RAMBLING VARIETIES
Rosa 'Albéric Barbier'
R. 'Albertine'
R. 'American Pillar'
R. banksiae 'Lutea'
R. 'Emily Gray'
R. 'Paul's Himalayan Musk'
R. 'Veilchenblau'
R. 'Wedding Day'

Rosa 'Golden Showers'

○ ◐ ◖ ⁞⁞ 🍂 ❖LATE SUMMER to EARLY AUTUMN
H 5m (16ft) S 3m (10ft)

This old favourite bears large, double yellow flowers throughout late summer and into early autumn. A valuable repeat-flowering climbing rose, it is suitable for any size of garden. Its continued popularity stems from its rain resistance and reliable flowering.

Rosa 'Handel'

○ ◐ ◖ ⁞⁞ 🍂 ❖LATE SUMMER to AUTUMN
H 3m (10ft) S 2.5m (8ft)

With its pink-edged cream flowers, produced during late summer and into autumn, this and other 'chocolate-box' roses aren't popular with those who follow fashion. The double, subtly scented blooms on this repeat-flowering climber are borne in clusters against handsome, glossy, bronze-tinted foliage. It is rain-resistant, but mildew and black spot can be a problem.

Rosa 'Madame Grégoire Staechelin'

H 6m (20ft) S 4m (13ft)
○ ◐ ◖ ⁞⁞ 🍂 ❖EARLY SUMMER, AUTUMN

Deliciously fragrant, this climbing rose bears double, crimson-flushed, pink, early-summer flowers that stand out against a backdrop of dark green leaves. There's added interest in autumn, when this lovely rose is decorated with bright red hips. It is ideal for covering arches and pergolas in sun or partial shade, or for east- or west-facing walls and fences.

Rosa 'Guinée'

○ ◐ ◖ ⁞⁞ 🍂 ❖MIDSUMMER
H 5m (16ft) S 2.5m (8ft)

Sumptuous, fragrant, double, blackish-red flowers, up to 10cm (4in) across, are produced during midsummer on this vigorous, repeat-flowering, climbing rose. Combine it with other 'bruised' colours in a sunny border by training it up trellis screens or use it as a backdrop. Watch out for mildew.

Rosa 'Madame Alfred Carrière'

○ ◐ ◖ ⁞⁞ 🍂 ❖MIDSUMMER to AUTUMN
H 5m (16ft) S 3m (10ft)

An old, repeat-flowering climbing rose, it bears fragrant, double, white or pale pink flowers from midsummer to autumn. The pliable stems are ideal for training and this rose is perfect for covering arches and pergolas in sun or partial shade, or for covering east-, west-, or north-facing vertical surfaces.

Rosa 'Maigold'

○ ◐ ◖ ⁞⁞ 🍂 ❖SUMMER, AUTUMN
H and S 2.5m (8ft)

Clusters of semi-double, bronze-yellow blooms are set off by the handsome foliage, even on very young plants. Flowering first in early summer, this deliciously fragrant climber produces a second flush of flowers in autumn. It is a very prickly rose that can be used along boundary fences to deter intruders.

Rosa 'Mermaid'
○ ◐ ◑ ‖ 🐛 ❖LATE SUMMER to AUTUMN
H and S 6m (20ft)

Give this strong-growing, repeat-flowering climbing rose space and it will reward you with masses of lovely, fragrant, single, primrose-yellow flowers throughout late summer and into autumn. Plant it against a large expanse of east- or west-facing wall that's sheltered from winter cold and once established it will romp away.

Rosa 'Mortimer Sackler'
○ ◐ ◑ ‖ 🐛 ❖SUMMER
H and S 3m (10ft)

Beautiful, fist-sized, open bowl-shaped flowers in a delicate shade of shell pink are borne on near-thornless stems. A lovely rose from bud to fully open flower, it is an excellent climber for covering sheltered, sunny walls and fences. It is also disease-resistant.

Rosa 'New Dawn'
○ ◐ ◑ ‖ 🐛 ❖LATE SUMMER to AUTUMN
H 3m (10ft) S 2.5m (8ft)

A versatile climber that produces lovely fragrant, double, pale pearl-pink flowers, it blooms throughout late summer and into autumn. It will produce a succession of small but perfectly formed blooms in abundance and is a good choice for all but north-facing walls and fences.

Rosa 'Paul's Himalayan Musk'
○ ◐ ◑ ‖ 🐛 ❖SUMMER
H and S 10m (33ft)

This outstanding rambler bears a succession of fabulous clusters of very fragrant, rosette-like, double, pale pink flowers throughout the summer. It is the perfect choice for training into a vigorous mature tree or for covering a sunny wall or fence.

Rosa 'Paul's Scarlet Climber'
○ ◐ ◑ ‖ 🐛 ❖EARLY SUMMER
H and S 3m (10ft)

Cover a sunny fence or wall with this vigorous climber that bears clusters of double, subtly fragrant, brilliant red flowers during early summer. The flowers, which last a month or more, tend to dull with age and the lustrous foliage is rather disease-prone. Less vigorous than many varieties, it's a good choice where space is restricted.

Rosa 'Rambling Rector'
○ ◐ ◑ ‖ 🐛 ❖SUMMER, AUTUMN
H and S 6m (20ft)

An uplifting sight in summer, this rambler produces huge clusters of fragrant, semi-double, creamy-coloured flowers on vigorous – some would say rampant – arching stems. The flowers are followed by small, rounded, red hips to extend the season of interest. Useful for covering large walls or fences or to camouflage an eyesore, it can be planted against a north-facing wall, but flowering will be reduced.

Rosa 'Schoolgirl'
○ ◑ ◌ ‖ 🍂 ❖LATE SUMMER to AUTUMN
H 3m (10ft) S 2.5m (8ft)

This unusual, repeat-flowering climbing rose remains popular for its fragrant, double, orange-apricot flowers that are borne during late summer and into the autumn. Use it to cover a sunny wall of your house or garage, or plant it behind an evergreen shrub, where its tendency to get leggy and leafless near the base as it matures will be disguised.

Rosa 'A Shropshire Lad'
○ ◑ ◌ ‖ 🍂 ❖SUMMER
H 2.5m (8ft) S 1.2m (4ft)

A super, thornless, climbing English rose, this bears peachy-pink to pale pink flowers with a rich, fruity fragrance. The flowers open out from tighter cup-shaped blooms into beautiful, many-petalled rosettes. The vigorous, disease-resistant growth is clothed with large, lustrous leaves.

Rosa 'Veilchenblau'
○ ◑ ◌ ‖ 🍂 ❖EARLY SUMMER
H and S 4m (13ft)

Orange-scented, semi-double, magenta to violet, early-summer flowers are each attractively streaked with white. The flowers, borne in clusters, fade gracefully to a greyish lilac. This thornless rambler is ideal for covering well-used arches and pergolas in sun or partial shade.

Rosa 'Wedding Day'
○ ◑ ◌ ‖ 🍂 ❖SUMMER
H 8m (26ft) S 4m (13ft)

This rampant rambler produces huge clusters of single, fragrant, creamy-coloured flowers throughout summer. It is a good choice if you want a single rose to cover a large expanse of south-, east- or west-facing wall, or perhaps to add seasonal interest to a vigorous mature tree.

Rosa 'Zéphirine Drouhin'
Thornless rose
○ ◑ ◌ ‖ 🍂 ❖LATE SUMMER to AUTUMN
H 3m (10ft) S 2m (6ft)

A lovely repeat-flowering Bourbon rose, its thornless stems are smothered in fragrant, double, deep-pink, late-summer flowers that continue into autumn. It's ideal for covering arches and pergolas in partial shade or for east-, west-, or north-facing walls and fences. The thorn-free foliage is a bonus.

Schisandra rubriflora
○ ◑ ◌ ‖ 🍂 ❖LATE SPRING, EARLY SUMMER
H 10m (33ft) S 4m (13ft)

An unusual twining climber, this has slender shoots and narrow, fresh green foliage, which sets off the stunning, pendent, deep-crimson blooms a treat. On female plants the flowers are followed by red fruits. It will be a talking point on a trellis next to the patio.

Schizophragma hydrangeoides
Japanese hydrangea vine
○ ◐ ◑ ● ♦ ‖ 🐝 ❖MIDSUMMER
H 12m (39ft) S 3m (10ft)

With cream-coloured midsummer flowers resembling those of the lacecap hydrangeas, this lovely vine is ideal for covering house and garden walls. It is slow to get going, but once it does, it can grow 50cm (20in) a year. It is ideal for planting against a large wall or fence in sun or shade.

Solanum crispum 'Glasnevin'
Chilean potato tree
○ ♦ ‖ 🐝 ❖SUMMER
H 6m (20ft) S 4m (13ft)

This reliable, fast-growing, evergreen or semi-evergeen climber is smothered in clusters of fragrant, lilac-purple, starry flowers all summer long. The flowers are followed by pale yellow fruits. A great choice for covering a sunny, sheltered wall or fence, it works particularly well as part of an informal planting scheme.

Solanum laxum 'Album'
Potato vine
○ ◐ ❄ ♦ ‖ ❖LATE SUMMER
H and S 6m (20ft)

Jasmine-scented, starry, white, late-summer flowers are borne in clusters on this lovely evergreen or semi-evergreen climber. The fragrant flowers are followed by rounded black fruits. It is a great choice for covering a sheltered wall or fence in milder parts of the country. In colder regions, grow it in a cool conservatory or greenhouse.

Sophora microphylla
○ ‖ ❖EARLY SPRING
H and S 3m (10ft)

Large, pendent, bell-shaped, yellow flowers hang from arching branches on this open, spreading evergreen shrub in spring. The flowers are long-lasting and eye-catching, but can look a bit tatty once the petals fall. It can be trained against a south-facing wall or fence. Good variety: 'Sun King' (dark yellow flowers; shown above).

Stauntonia hexaphylla
○ ◐ ❄ ♦ ‖ ❖SPRING
H and S 3m (10ft)

Plant this quick-growing evergreen climber against a sunny, sheltered wall outside or in a cool greenhouse or conservatory. It bears dainty clusters of fragrant, purple-flushed, pinky-white flowers on cherry-like stalks. If pollinated, female plants bear purple fruits.

Thunbergia alata
Black-eyed Susan
○ ❄ ♦ ‖ ❖LATE SUMMER to AUTUMN
H 2m (6ft) S 1m (40in)

This tender, evergreen perennial climber is normally grown as an annual. Its pretty, trumpet-shaped flowers, in orange, yellow or creamy vanilla, each have a chocolate-coloured eye. Blooming throughout late summer until the first frost, it can be used to provide instant colour while more permanent climbers are getting established.

Trachelospermum asiaticum

SUMMER

H 6m (20ft) S 3m (10ft)

This twining, woody, evergreen climber produces clusters of jasmine-scented, creamy-coloured, starry flowers from midsummer onwards. Grow it up a sheltered, sunny wall or use it to scramble through a strongly growing tree in mild regions. In areas with cold winters, grow this climber in a cool conservatory or a greenhouse.

Trachelospermum jasminoides

Star jasmine

SUMMER

H 9m (30ft) S 3m (10ft)

A fashionable plant, this lovely, fragrant, evergreen climber deserves to be grown even more widely. From midsummer it is covered in clusters of jasmine-scented, starry, white flowers. Use it to decorate a sheltered, sunny wall in mild areas. In cold regions, it can be grown in a cool conservatory or greenhouse.

Tropaeolum majus Nasturtium

LATE SUMMER

H and S 1.5m (5ft)

Quick and easy to grow, this annual climber produces charming, spurred, funnel-shaped flowers in shades of red, orange and yellow throughout late summer, over attractive, scalloped, wavy-edged leaves. It is a useful filler for instant cover on newly planted walls and fences. It also provides a hot splash of colour for container schemes.

Tropaeolum peregrinum

Canary creeper

MIDSUMMER to EARLY AUTUMN

H and S 3m (10ft)

Brilliant yellow, finely fringed flowers with hooked spurs stand out against the very attractive, five-lobed, greyish-green leaves on this lovely creeper. It blooms from midsummer into early autumn. Although an annual, it self-seeds freely, to reappear the following year. It's useful for scrambling over low walls and chain-link fences in sunny spots.

Tropaeolum speciosum

Flame creeper

MIDSUMMER to EARLY AUTUMN

H and S 3m (10ft)

The lovely, long-spurred, flaming-red flowers of this creeper bloom from midsummer and into early autumn and are followed by bead-like blue fruits. Its roots like to be deep in humus-rich soil and well shaded, its flowers in sun or partial shade, so it's perfect for growing through shrubs and trees.

Vitis 'Brant'

pH→ –pH↑ AUTUMN

H 9m (30ft) S 2m (6ft)

This is a vigorous vine that will clothe a sunny structure with bright green, classically lobed leaves that turn fiery shades of red and orange during the autumn. The sprigs of green grapes produced in summer swell and ripen to black by the autumn, but the fruits tend to have a lot of pips.

Vitis coignetiae
Crimson glory vine
○ ◑ ‖ pH→ –pH↑ ❖AUTUMN
H 15m (49ft) S 5m (16ft)

A vigorous vine with impressive, heart-shaped leaves up to 30cm (12in) long, it will cloak any vertical surface with foliage. In autumn, when the leaves turn fiery shades of red, accompanied by small, blue-black, inedible grapes, it really takes centre stage. This is a super vine for a sheltered and sunny brick wall.

Vitis vinifera 'Schiava Grossa' (syn. 'Black Hamburgh')
○ ◑ ‖ pH→ –pH↑ ❖AUTUMN
H 7m (23ft) S 3m (10ft)

This vigorous, hardy grapevine can be grown indoors or outdoors. It needs a warm, sheltered, south-facing wall or can be trained over a sturdy pergola. The large leaves offer a shady retreat in a hot summer and in autumn it will reward you with large bunches of sweet, blue-black grapes. Routine pruning and training will be needed.

Wisteria × formosa
○ ◑ ‖ ❖EARLY SUMMER
H 9m (30ft) S 5m (16ft)

This is a vigorous, twining climber that produces eye-catching pendent strings, up to 25cm (10in) long, of fragrant, violet-blue flowers during early summer, followed in warm summers by velvety seedpods up to 15cm (6in) long. A versatile climber, it makes an excellent show on a house wall or on a pergola and looks superb in a Mediterranean or cottage-garden setting.

Vitis vinifera 'Purpurea'
Grapevine
○ ◑ ‖ pH→ –pH↑ ❖AUTUMN
H 7m (23ft) S 2m (6ft)

The leaves on this ornamental climber emerge grey-green with pink tinges and mature to deep red. By the time small, inedible, purple grapes are produced in autumn, the leaves have turned deep purple. Grow it along a sunny wall or fence or over a sturdy pergola.

Wisteria floribunda
Japanese wisteria
○ ◑ ‖ ❖EARLY SUMMER, AUTUMN
H 9m (30ft) S 5m (16ft)

During early summer, striking 30cm (12in) long strings of fragrant, violet, blue, pink or white flowers are produced on this vigorous twining climber. In warm summers these are followed by velvety seedpods. The attractive foliage turns yellow in autumn. This climber looks superb growing on a house wall or over a pergola. Good variety: 'Rosea' (rose-pink flowers).

Wisteria sinensis 'Alba'
Chinese wisteria
○ ◑ ◗ ‖ ❖EARLY SUMMER
H 9m (30ft) S 5m (16ft)

Glorious, pendent strings, up to 30cm (12in) long, of fragrant, white flowers are produced during early summer on this climber, followed in warm summers by velvety pods up to 15cm (6in) long. It is highly versatile and makes a wonderful display on a house wall or over a pergola, or you could try it as an unusual weeping standard. Good variety: 'Prolific' (lilac-blue flowers).

Challenging sites

Most climbers and wall shrubs are accommodating plants that cope with conditions other plants might find somewhat difficult. There are plenty to choose from and, with a little thought, you can find a climber to cope with the most challenging situation – hot and dry or cold and shady. They are useful characters too; they throw themselves at the matter in hand, whether it is covering a steep bank, disguising an ugly building or scrambling up a high wall.

Shady walls

Which climber you choose for a shady situation will depend on how heavily shaded it is: does it get any sun at all and, if so, how much? If there are no neighbouring buildings or trees casting additional shade, aspect will be the major influence on your choice. North-facing walls and fences get little or no sun at all, east-facing ones get morning sun, and those that are west-facing get afternoon and evening rays.

Partially shaded walls

If a wall or fence gets a few hours' direct sun, you have a much wider choice of climbers than if it were in full shade, whether that sun is in the morning or later in the day. For example, most roses will perform and flower well provided they get four hours or more of sun every day in the growing season. As the sun moves around, different forces come into play to cast their shadow, and these can change dramatically with the time of the year. A wall or fence that gets some sun at midday in summer might be in total shade in winter. However, as deciduous climbers are dormant at that time, and evergreens nearly so, shade in winter may not be a problem.

Another challenge that climbers face is that the soil at the base of a wall or fence can be very dry because the ground is sheltered from rain. This is particularly a problem when the wall faces east. So do not plant too close.

Easterly aspects are also very cold and prone to freezing conditions. Coupled with the thawing effect of the morning sun, this can be very damaging, especially to plants, like camellias, that are unwise enough to bloom at such a treacherous time.

Like most roses, 'Albertine' will grow and flower happily on a partially shaded wall: it needs only a few hours of sun at some point in the day during the growing season.

A frost-proof wall shrub

The blooms of the flowering quince (*Chaenomeles*) are frost-proof. This vigorous wall shrub carries striking, yet delicate-looking, spring flowers that last until early summer on spiny branches, followed by aromatic yellow-green fruits in autumn. Look out for: *Chaenomeles* x *superba* 'Crimson and Gold' (deep red with golden stamens) and *Chaenomeles speciosa* 'Geisha Girl' (apricot-pink) and 'Moerloosei' (pale pink).

Ivies are far from dull. *Hedera colchica* 'Sulphur Heart' adds light and all-year interest to any heavily shaded spot.

Walls in deep shade

The much-maligned ivies are the obvious choice for heavily shaded walls. They're well adapted to the competition for light and water that mature trees impose, so a shady wall

Once established, the climbing hydrangea is a reliable performer, with delicately lacy flowerheads.

or fence is not that challenging. Many gardeners consider ivies to be destructive, invasive thugs, but they do provide some wonderful foliage that looks good throughout the year. Always pick a well-grown plant, which will thrive, rather than a weedier individual that will struggle.

The large-leaved variegated forms of *Hedera colchica* are excellent and have spectacular foliage. *Hedera colchica* 'Dentata Variegata', with pale-edged foliage, is one of the best. It is a big grower ultimately, so if you want something smaller try *Hedera helix* 'Glacier', which has soft-green and white leaves.

Often thought of as shrubs for ground cover, *Euonymus fortunei* varieties make brilliant short climbers up to 3m (10ft) and thrive in heavy shade. *Euonymus fortunei*

'Emerald Gaiety' has small, green and white variegated leaves, which show up well in shade.

If you're after flowers, try the climbing hydrangea (*Hydrangea anomala* subsp. *petiolaris*). This is a self-clinger with lacecap heads of creamy-white flowers in summer. It drops its leaves in winter, but the brown stems are not unattractive. For winter interest, team it with a small-leaved ivy.

Boston ivy (*Parthenocissus tricuspidata* 'Veitchii') and Virginia creeper (*Parthenocissus quinquefolia*) are both happy in heavy shade. However, their autumn tints will be more magnificent if they get some sun. They're a good choice if a rampant plant is needed – once they start, there is no stopping them.

Planting shady passageways

A shady passageway is a real challenge because, as well as low light levels and dry soil, there are often buffeting wind currents too. Ivies are probably the best adapted to growing in these circumstances, and those with variegated or pale foliage will add much-needed light and colour.

More plants for heavily shaded walls

Cotoneaster horizontalis
Garrya elliptica
Hedera helix 'Goldchild'
Jasminum nudiflorum
Pileostegia viburnoides
Pyracantha 'Orange Glow'
Schizophragma hydrangeoides

High walls

Large expanses of masonry cry out for the softening effects of foliage. Although a high wall or fence may seem daunting to the average plant, a vigorous climber or tall-growing wall shrub will relish the challenge. Strong-growing climbers are adapted to scaling large trees and rock faces – they need to get to the top to get the light. Climbing a high wall is all in a day's work.

Vigorous climbers

Wisterias look splendid growing against high walls – their flower panicles are shown to advantage, and their network of woody stems gradually develops into a living sculpture over the years.

On a similar scale, the spectacular crimson glory vine (*Vitis coignetiae*) will scale a two-storey house in the second or third season. The huge vine leaves give an exotic effect and colour richly in shades of gold and flame in autumn.

On large walls where providing a support is a problem, it may be better to plant a wall shrub than a vigorous climber. Few shrubs are more arresting than *Magnolia grandiflora*, with its opulent flowers. The variety 'Exmouth' flowers at a young age and grows quickly.

Supports and maintenance

Self-clinging climbers such as ivy and Virginia creeper (*Parthenocissus*) can make their own way up a high wall or fence, attaching their stems to the surface using modified root suckers. You might need to help them get going with low wires or wall nails, but then they will be fine on their own. Other climbers and wall shrubs need something to cling to or something you can anchor them to, to stop them falling off. The best solution is strong wires fixed to the wall with galvanized vine-eyes (*see* pages 50–1).

Wall trellis is no good for vigorous, woody climbers. It will all too quickly be smothered and with time will deteriorate. Don't ever try to grow wisteria up it!

When choosing a climber for a high wall, consider how you'll prune it. A really vigorous rose, such as the rambler 'Paul's Himalayan Musk', will certainly cover a huge area, but when you get up there to prune it you'll regret your choice, as it will have scrambled all over the place. Instead, it's better to pick a more contained variety, such as 'Madame Alfred Carrière'.

More plants for high walls

Actinidia deliciosa

Clematis montana

Fremontodendron californicum

Hydrangea serratifolia

Parthenocissus tricuspidata 'Veitchii'

Passiflora caerulea

Rosa 'Félicité Perpétue'

Rosa 'Sander's White Rambler'

Wisteria floribunda

Wisteria sinensis

Don't forget

When choosing a climber or wall shrub, bear in mind that if the site is inaccessible, you need one that will not require regular pruning or training. A self-clinging climber might be best.

Wisteria floribunda: a well-established wisteria is a truly magnificent sight in full bloom, and in winter the twining branches can be just as remarkable.

In nearly all gardens there is something you'd rather not look at: an oil tank, a wheelie bin, a washing line or a garden shed. Maybe your neighbour's house or garage wall is bleak and unappealing? The tendency is to plant a hedge or screening shrubs, or even a tree. All do their job, but they take up space and time to grow. Climbers offer a quick, space-saving solution.

Creating a screen
Sturdy trellis panels supported by fence posts are easy to install and provide a stout support for twining climbers that grow quickly to cover them. Large-leaved ivies, such as *Hedera algeriensis* 'Gloire de Marengo', provide evergreen cover and grow quickly once they get going. Evergreen honeysuckles, such as *Lonicera similis* var. *delavayi* and the ever-popular *Lonicera japonica* 'Halliana', have the bonus of fragrant summer flowers and thrive in sun or shade. Where there is a reasonable amount of light, you could mix a honeysuckle with a light, late-flowering clematis such as *Clematis* 'Royal Velours'. In a sunny spot

Rampant climbers will do an efficient job of disguising an obtrusive garage.

Trachelospermum jasminoides will in time provide a dense evergreen screen, with the bonus of fragrant white flowers in summer and red winter foliage.

Hiding a neighbour's building
A neighbour's building can overpower a garden. You want to hide it, but a conifer hedge is not necessarily the answer; it will need cutting and it will take up a strip a couple of metres wide along the edge of your garden. One simple solution is to use heavy pergola posts in a line down the boundary, with a single row of rafters along the top. Grow vigorous climbers such as *Rosa* 'Paul's Himalayan Musk', *Rosa* 'Seagull' or *Actinidia kolomikta* up the posts and over the rafters, and that building will soon disappear. Or how about using ropes draped between the posts? You can tie the roses or other climbers into these and create garlands of flowers that will hide those horrors.

Trellis panels covered in climbers will make an effective screen for a wheelie bin.

Smothering an ugly building
A rampant climber will throw itself up an ugly building and over the roof, and in a year or two you'll have a mound of foliage and flowers. Be warned: many fast-growing climbers become weighty and can cause weak structures to collapse. *Rosa* 'Rambling Rector' is a good choice, with masses of white flowers in summer. *Rosa filipes* 'Kiftsgate' is an option, but it does get very big. A rampant rose is not a wise choice if you need access to the building – and never, ever grow it on an oil tank!

In a naturalistic setting, consider the Russian vine (*Fallopia baldschuanica*) – a thug, but its tiny white flowers are not unattractive. Or try *Vitis coignetiae*, *Clematis montana* or *Clematis armandii*.

Don't forget
When planting climbers next to a stump, set the rootball about 50cm (20in) away and train stems towards it. If necessary, cover the stump with fine netting, to give the plant a foothold.

Low walls

We tend to think of climbers as plants that grow up and cover tall objects. However, they're also very useful for clothing low structures, such as retaining walls and low dividing walls. Maybe you live in a bungalow and have limited wall space? In such situations, climbers still have an important role to play, but you want plants that grow laterally, and do not get too tall.

Don't forget

Although these low climbers do not have a great height to scale, you might still need to encourage them to scramble. Train the shoots onto the wall using wall nails, or plastic mesh anchored loosely to the top and sides of the wall near where the climber is planted.

Scramblers not ramblers

To clothe low walls you need those climbers that scramble across the ground, or over low shrubs, rather than mountaineers that scale trees. If you want an evergreen, consider a small-leaved ivy, a variety of *Hedera helix*. This is the common English ivy, which scrambles around on the forest floor before growing up a tree trunk. There are many attractive forms. *Hedera helix* 'Oro di Bogliasco' (formerly 'Goldheart') has dark green leaves with golden centres. It's a good choice to clothe unattractive low walls, such as those made from concrete blocks, to which it will cling with tenacity. An alternative would be *Euonymus fortunei*, a short climber that is happy in sun or shade.

Some clematis grow particularly well against low walls. The varieties of *Clematis alpina* and *Clematis macropetala* are especially attractive in late spring, with dainty, many-petalled flowers in shades of pink, blue and white. Their twining stems and the elegant posture of their blooms make them ideal for the edge of a terrace or alongside steps.

Most roses appreciate a little more height than is offered by a low wall or fence, but there are some short climbers, such as 'Aloha', which grows to around 2–2.5m (6–8ft) and is just like a tall bush rose. Also, the patio climbers are good here. 'Warm Welcome', with orange-red flowers and dark red-green leaves, is lovely and great for a low wall in full sun.

Honeysuckles clothe the forest floor before scrambling through shrubs and scaling trees, too. Any variety of the common honeysuckle (*Lonicera periclymenum*) will clamber over a low wall or fence. They do tend to get twiggy with dead wood as they age, so cut them back after flowering every couple of years.

More climbers for low walls

Clematis cirrhosa 'Wisley Cream'
Clematis 'Frances Rivis'
Euonymus fortunei 'Silver Queen'
Hedera helix 'Goldchild'
Hedera helix 'Sagittifolia'
Lonicera × brownii 'Dropmore Scarlet'
Rhodochiton atrosanguineus
Rosa 'Laura Ford'
Rosa 'The Pilgrim'

Honeysuckle and *Clematis* 'Ville de Lyon' scramble together through a decorative trellis set on a low brick wall to make an attractive screen or divider.

Dry, hot spots

If you're lucky enough to have a sunny south- or west-facing garden, you might well have a dry, hot spot that basks in sunshine at some point in the summer. This is challenging for some plants, but it does give you the chance to grow the more tender sun-lovers that would shiver in colder conditions.

When choosing climbers and wall shrubs for dry, hot spots, look for drought-tolerant plants. These often have leaves that are silver, small and leathery or hairy – all adaptations that help reduce water loss. Plants that hail from the Mediterranean are the order of the day, and many of these have bright, exotic-looking blooms that will shine in the sun.

Sun-loving wall shrubs

When you think about it, there are few trees in hot, dry climates and, therefore, few climbers. There is a wider choice of wall shrubs that are adapted to these conditions.

The colourful orange-red trumpet vine Campsis × tagliabuana 'Madame Galen' is stunning when draped over the top of a pergola in full sun.

California lilacs (*Ceanothus*) are an obvious choice. The evergreen varieties are the most spectacular blue-flowering shrubs we grow in our gardens. They're not the hardiest creatures, so will appreciate the shelter of a fence or wall. The vigorous, large-leaved *Ceanothus arboreus* 'Trewithen Blue' is magnificent – but it does need plenty of room. The sky-blue flowers look beautiful against the shiny emerald leaves in spring to early summer. Of the small-leaved varieties, *Ceanothus* 'Concha' and 'Puget Blue' are excellent, both producing masses of sapphire flowers that practically obscure the leaves. Ceanothus are not long-lived, so be prepared to replace them after eight or ten years. Although they grow on alkaline soils, they might struggle on shallow chalk.

The pineapple broom (*Cytisus battandieri*), so named because of the delicious fruity fragrance of its flowers, loves chalk and grows quickly to 5m (16ft) or more. The stems and leaves are silvery grey,

The broom *Cytisus battandieri* is a fast-growing wall shrub with silver leaves and pineapple-scented flowers.

Fruit for hot, sunny spots

A hot, sunny wall or fence makes the ideal home for trained fruit. Peaches and apricots can be fan-trained on a wired wall, and once established will crop well. The flowers are protected from frost, and the fruit has sun to ripen it.

For something easier, choose a fig. Figs have splendid large, architectural leaves and produce a good crop of fruits in late summer in sheltered situations. 'Brown Turkey' is the most popular variety.

A fruiting grapevine will thrive on a warm, sunny wall provided it has wires. Care is easy: prune in early winter to a framework of main stems. The foliage is attractive, and crops can be heavy of both dessert and wine varieties.

More plants for dry, hot spots

Billardiera
Carpenteria californica
Clematis cirrhosa var. *balearica*
Clematis florida var. *sieboldiana*
Clianthus puniceus
Eccremocarpus scaber
Jasminum × stephanense
Passiflora caerulea
Sollya heterophylla
Trachelospermum asiaticum
Vitis vinifera 'Purpurea'

and the rich yellow flowers are produced in large heads in mid- and late summer. Also, try *Cytisus battandieri* 'Yellow Tail', which is more compact and free-flowering.

Fremontodendron 'California Glory' is another tall grower, with silver-backed leaves and large, cup-shaped golden flowers. It needs a high wall or fence, so is ideal against the

Don't forget

In most gardens the driest soil is invariably at the base of walls – the foundations will draw out moisture and, if a building has overhanging eaves, rainwater will not reach the border.

Solanum crispum 'Glasnevin' is a very versatile plant. It thrives in dry, hot sites and copes with moist soil too.

south-facing gable-end of the house. It makes a good partner for *Solanum crispum* 'Glasnevin', a scrambling shrubby climber with large heads of lilac-blue flowers. Each flower has reflexed petals and a pointed yellow beak, which picks up the colour of the fremontodendron.

Many abutilons lend themselves to training against a wall, particularly those with fine, lax stems that need support. 'Kentish Belle' is a popular choice, with semi-evergreen foliage and hanging lantern blooms of brick red and gold. *Abutilon megapotamicum* 'Variegatum' is an old favourite, with narrow, green leaves blotched with gold and dainty hanging bells of yellow and red.

Sun-loving climbers

The trumpet vine (*Campsis*) is a rampant climber with arching stems and attractive green foliage. In late summer and early autumn, the trumpet-shaped flowers are produced at the tips of the shoots,

so don't tidy this plant up halfway through the growing season. *Campsis × tagliabuana* 'Madame Galen' is the finest variety, producing large, apricot-orange flowers in generous clusters. Campsis is partially self-clinging, but needs some form of support to prevent collapse.

Jasmines are also a good choice for hot, sheltered sites, where their perfume will be at its best. *Jasminum officinale* 'Affine' is a popular white jasmine, with scented flowers in summer and autumn and dark green, fern-like foliage. In favoured locations, it's well worth trying the less hardy *Jasminum polyanthum*. It has fine, twining stems, dark green leaves and heavily scented white blooms in spring that will conjure up images of Mediterranean nights under the stars.

Damp soil

Well-drained, fertile soil that never dries out provides the ideal growing conditions for most plants. However, when soil is continuously waterlogged, few plants cope with the lack of air around their roots. As ever, it's all about choosing plants that have the best chance of success. If you can improve the drainage of a site, the choice of what you can grow increases.

More plants for damp sites

Akebia quinata
Clematis montana 'Grandiflora'
Hydrangea serratifolia
Lonicera sempervirens
Pyracantha 'Orange Glow'
Solanum crispum 'Glasnevin'
Solanum laxum
Wisteria sinensis

Climbers for damp sites

Wisterias prefer a moist soil and will grow happily unless the soil is really waterlogged. As they're capable of putting on a lot of growth where they have room to expand, the copious foliage will draw a lot of moisture from the soil in the growing season. This is a useful way to dry out the ground around a pergola for the benefit of plants that like drier soil.

Most honeysuckles cope with quite moist soils. Being woodland plants, they will grow better if the soil is enriched with compost, which in itself will improve the structure. You can try any variety of *Lonicera periclymenum* or *Lonicera japonica.*

Solanums, especially *Solanum crispum*, is very happy in damp soil and produces good foliage as well as copious flowers. The climbing hydrangea (*Hydrangea anomala* subsp. *petiolaris*) is also fairly tolerant of wet conditions.

Vigorous clematis, such as *Clematis montana* and *Clematis flammula,* also do well on permanently moist soil, as will the native *Clematis vitalba* – a good one for a naturalistic garden.

Improving damp soil

Soil at the base of a wall or fence can be damaged during construction. Heavy clay soils get very compacted by builders and their machines. If this is the problem, deep digging and forking through the subsoil might put the matter right, especially if you incorporate some coarse grit and well-rotted manure.

If the site is just generally wet, you might be able to raise the soil level where you want to plant, perhaps by constructing a simple raised bed from timber sleepers and filling it with good topsoil. If you're doing this adjacent to the house, be careful not to pile soil against the brickwork above the damp course.

Don't forget

On wet soils, try to plant in spring rather than autumn. This avoids the shrub or climber having permanently wet feet through the winter, when it is dormant.

The common honeysuckle (*Lonicera periclymenum*) is a tough woodland plant that grows perfectly well on moist, humus-rich soils.

Sandy soil

Sandy soils are usually very well drained but low in nutrients because they get washed away when the rainwater passes through; also, they can dry out quickly. While this is a problem for some plants, many don't mind these conditions. The advantage of sandy soils is that they warm up quickly, so tender plants are less likely to suffer in winter. Also, they're easy to dig, even after rainfall.

Plants that succeed

If the situation is sunny, most plants that like hot, dry conditions (*see* page 112) will do well on sandy soils. In favoured areas, especially by the coast, exotics like the crimson bottlebrush (*Callistemon citrinus* 'Splendens') are an option. With its lax branches and narrow, olive-green leaves, this Australian shrub is easy to grow and spectacular when it produces its fluffy, scarlet flowers in summer. The secret of success is to trim branches back to behind the flowerheads once the blooms fade.

The lobster claw (*Clianthus puniceus*) enjoys similar conditions.

The grapevine *Vitis* 'Brant' grows well on sandy soil and produces sweet, aromatic fruits when the foliage colours richly in autumn.

It sprawls across rocks and the ground in its native habitat, but is easily trained against a sunny wall, where its scarlet, black-eyed flowers are shown to perfection.

Grapes, both ornamental and fruiting, do well on sandy soils in sunny situations. *Vitis* 'Brant' is generally regarded as ornamental for its large vine leaves that colour beautifully in autumn. It does, however, produce small, palatable fruits, particularly in a hot summer. It is a vigorous plant: prune it only in early winter, once the leaves have fallen. *Vitis vinifera* 'Purpurea' is smaller in stature and has wonderful, grey-green, pink-tinged new leaves that turn soft purple with age.

Many clematis seem to struggle on sandy soils, sometimes due to acid conditions, but more often due to drought before the plants are established. The evergreen *Clematis armandii* does better than most.

Improving sandy soil

Sandy soils are easily improved by the addition of organic matter in the form of well-rotted manure or good garden compost. This increases the humus content, which helps to retain nutrients and water between the large mineral sand particles. Where soil is particularly sandy, it is worth adding some loam-based John Innes compost to the planting hole and its surroundings. This increases the amount of small soil particles, also helping to retain water and nutrients. Add slow-release fertilizer when planting a new climber and remember to reapply annually. Watering will be essential during the first growing season.

Don't forget

Sandy soils can be, and often are, acidic. It is worth checking the pH of your soil before you plant a clematis, which prefers more alkaline conditions (see page 45).

More plants for sandy soil

Ampelopsis brevipedunculata var. *maximowiczii* 'Elegans'
Campsis radicans
Ceanothus 'Concha'
Hedera helix 'Oro di Bogliasco'
Humulus lupulus 'Aureus'
Jasminum officinale f. *affine*
Trachelospermum jasminoides
Vitis coignetiae

Clay soil

Everyone who gardens on clay soil moans about it, because it's heavy and difficult to dig, and can be wet in winter. However, plants generally love it: it holds water efficiently, is rich in nutrients, and provides a firm footing. If your soil is clay, consider yourself lucky because you can grow a wider range of climbers and wall shrubs than those gardening on many other soil types. And this includes roses, which adore heavy clay and reward with vigorous growth and plenty of flowers.

Climbing roses are a natural choice to grow on clay soils. Trained well and fed regularly, they provide a wonderful display.

Choosing plants for clay

All roses do well on clay, so they're a natural choice where you want a flowering climber. They will grow in sun, or partial shade if there are a few hours of sunshine each day. Some varieties do better on shady walls than others (*see* page 107). Climbing roses are usually less vigorous than ramblers, so are a better choice for walls and fences up to 2m (6ft) in height. All need support: this is best achieved with horizontal wires, which the rose stems can be tied into. Bending the stems and tying them horizontally encourages flowering sideshoots.

Pyracantha, cotoneaster and flowering quince (*Chaenomeles*) are all good wall shrubs for clay soils. Pyracantha and cotoneaster have the benefit of white flowers in spring, which are attractive to pollinating insects, and berries in autumn, which are loved by birds.

Flowering quince is valuable for its delicate blooms in early spring and its quince-like fruits in autumn. The flowers, which are borne on angular naked stems, have a wonderfully oriental air, and are a delight to cut for the house. Colours can be delicate, as in the apple-blossom pink and white blooms of *Chaenomeles speciosa* 'Moerloosei', or vivid, as in *Chaenomeles × superba* 'Crimson and Gold'.

More plants for clay soil

Actinidia kolomikta
Clematis viticella
Cotoneaster horizontalis
Fallopia baldschuanica
Parthenocissus henryana
Pyracantha 'Saphyr Rouge'
Rosa 'Albéric Barbier'
Rosa 'Teasing Georgia'
Wisteria floribunda

Improving clay soil

Clay soil can be improved by the addition of coarse horticultural grit. This helps to break up the solid structure of all those fine particles that cling together and make it sticky and heavy. Plenty of organic matter boosts the humus content in the soil, again helping to separate those fine clay particles. If both are applied in autumn, when the ground has been dug over, they will work their way into the soil during winter. Adding lime to a clay soil before planting also helps to break up its solid structure. This is particularly valuable on acid clay soils if you want to grow clematis.

Don't forget

Clay soils are nutrient-rich, but to ensure roses have enough magnesium, iron and potash for plenty of flowers and healthy growth, feed them with a rose fertilizer twice a year.

Chalky soil

Some plants, particularly ericaceous ones like camellias, cannot be grown on chalky soils. The alkalinity makes certain essential nutrients unavailable to them. However, most climbers and wall shrubs do not fall into this category, so the range of plants available is actually huge. You're spoilt for choice. And this includes the queen of climbers – clematis.

Plants for chalky soil

Chalky soil is not essential for clematis but they do thrive on it, so they're an obvious choice. It's still a good idea to incorporate plenty of organic matter prior to planting, as this helps to retain moisture. Dig over the soil as deeply as possible: clematis (particularly the large-flowered types) benefit from being planted 15cm (6in) deeper than when growing in their pots (*see* page 48). This helps develop plenty of shoots below ground level and aids recovery in case of wilt (*see* page 71). In sunny spots it's best to plant clematis behind another shrub, or put stones on the soil surface to shade the roots.

Most California lilacs (*Ceanothus*) do well on chalk and reward with their glorious blue flowers in spring, summer and autumn. The deciduous varieties are often overlooked in favour of evergreen ones, which is a pity. *Ceanothus* × *delileanus* 'Gloire de Versailles', for example, is a light, airy plant with loose heads of sky-blue flowers; they bloom twice, between midsummer and autumn.

For shady sites on chalk, all ivies succeed, as do *Euonymus fortunei* varieties, which make valuable short climbers. And there is the ever-useful *Cotoneaster horizontalis,* or *Cotoneaster atropurpureus* 'Variegatus', with its cream-variegated leaves and big red berries on herringbone branches.

Chalky soils warm up quickly in spring and are rarely waterlogged in winter so, in favoured locations, you might succeed with many of the more tender climbers and wall shrubs from the Mediterranean region (*see* pages 112–13).

Improving chalky soil

Chalky soils are improved by adding organic matter, particularly well-rotted farmyard manure, because the acidity helps neutralize the alkalinity. They can be low in nutrients, because the underlying chalk is free-draining and nutrients wash away with rainfall and watering. An annual application of slow-release general fertilizer in spring helps to compensate.

Don't forget

Chalky soils can be very dry. You may need to water fast-growing climbers, particularly in the first year. Mulching with compost or gravel helps conserve moisture and keep roots cool.

More plants for chalky soil

Ceanothus 'Puget Blue'
Clematis armandii
Clematis 'The President'
Cytisus battandieri
Euonymus fortunei 'Silver Queen'
Fremontodendron 'California Glory'
Jasminum officinale
Lonicera periclymenum 'Serotina'
Piptanthus nepalensis

Ceanothus make spectacular wall shrubs for sunny sites on most chalky soils. There are evergreen and deciduous forms.

Season by season

No matter how long you've been gardening, it's always useful to have a memory jogger to remind you of the most important tasks of the year. In the case of climbers and wall shrubs, it's vital that pruning and training are done at the right time: get it wrong and you could spoil the display for the following year and maybe even risk losing the plant altogether. It's also useful to know when to be alert for pest and disease threats so that any necessary action can be taken promptly. And of course it's good to know when is the best time to plant new specimens, take cuttings, sow seed, protect vulnerable plants – and do all the other routine but essential tasks that keep every gardener busy.

Spring

In early spring, the days are beginning to lengthen and it's a pleasure to get out into the garden and enjoy some fresh air. There's pruning to be done, and mulching and feeding, and it's time to sow annual climbers and plant container-grown climbers and wall shrubs – and to get one step ahead of those pests that fancy tasty young shoots.

Pruning

In early spring, before new growth gets underway, prune group 2 clematis (*see* pages 59 and 83); this includes large-flowered varieties that bloom in late spring or early summer and often produce a second flush in late summer. Also, prune group 3 clematis (*see* pages 59 and 84); these varieties flower later in the season, from summer into autumn. You can also renovate

Spend a bit of time pruning climbers on your pergola in spring and soon enough you'll be rewarded with a wonderful mass of colour.

overgrown evergreen wall shrubs by pruning just as they start to put on new growth. Shrubs that respond to hard pruning, like ivies and honeysuckle, can be cut back to a knee-high stubby framework; or take out one stem in three.

In late spring, prune group 1 clematis after flowering if necessary (*see* pages 59 and 78); these flower from midwinter into early spring and include varieties of *Clematis alpina, armandii, macropetala* and *montana*.

When cutting out old stems from a clematis, take care not to harm the delicate new shoots.

Sow seeds

In early spring you can start sowing seeds of annual climbers such as morning glory (*Ipomoea purpurea*), sweet pea (*Lathyrus odoratus*) and nasturtium (*Tropaeolum majus*). Sow in trays under cover and once the seedlings are large enough to handle transfer them into individual pots (*see* page 67). In late spring, when the plants have got going, harden them off in a cold frame, ready for planting out after all danger of frost has passed.

The evergreen *Clematis armandii* flowers in early to mid-spring. Remove any dead stems and leaves that might mar its beauty, but otherwise let it do its own thing.

Don't forget

Position new nesting boxes for birds in climbers and wall shrubs in early spring, while there is less pressure on your time in the garden. It is also worth cleaning out existing boxes, if you didn't complete this job in the autumn.

material, such as garden compost or composted bark. It will help to retain soil moisture, suppress weeds and keep the roots cool in summer. However, take care not to pile the mulch around the stems.

Pest alert

Protect new shoots of climbers by baiting, trapping or hand-picking slugs and snails. You can also put up slug-proof barriers, such as a layer of grit or copper rings, around vulnerable plants. Keep a look out for embryonic colonies of aphids at the soft shoot-tips of honeysuckles and clematis, and check the foliage for any signs of mildew. Take steps to eliminate any problems you find (*see* pages 68–71).

When you're planting a new climber against a fence post, make sure the roots are clear of any concrete around the foot of the post.

Give plants a head start

Plant new climbers and wall shrubs that have been raised in containers. For most clematis, choose a spot where their tops are in the sun and their roots are in the shade. Water climbers in dry soil regularly, even if it rains. Remember that climbers planted next to houses are often in the rain shadow of the overhanging roof, so do not feel the benefit of rain. Feed established climbers and wall shrubs with a slow-release balanced fertilizer, especially if they need to put on more growth to cover their support. For flowering climbers that have covered their support, use a high-potash fertilizer such as rose feed to encourage the production of more flowers. Don't forget to feed plants in containers. Give them a liquid feed while watering or add a slow-release fertilizer to the compost, which will feed the plants throughout the whole season. Mulch all climbers and wall shrubs with a generous layer of well-rotted organic

Copper rings can be effective at fending off slugs. Put them in place at the time of planting. Here they are used to protect young sweet peas.

Summer

With roses, honeysuckle, clematis and jasmine in full bloom, you'll want to spend long days and balmy evenings just sitting and admiring. If there are dry periods, however, you need to keep new climbers and wall shrubs well watered, and you should check all your climbers and wall shrubs to make sure that new growth is well supported and new stems are tied in. Be vigilant, as ever, for diseases. Note places where you could add interest with a new climber or wall shrub. Maybe you could propagate a few of your favourite plants.

Rosa 'American Pillar' is a glorious, rampant rambler that is at its peak in midsummer. Cut back the flowering stems once the blooms have faded.

Making new plants

Layer low and flexible stems now to make new plants (*see* page 66 and below). Suitable climbers for layering include clematis, ivies, climbing hydrangea, jasmine, *Akebia*, *Campsis*, *Vitis* and *Parthenocissus*.

In early summer, take softwood cuttings of *Actinidia*, honeysuckles and jasmine and many evergreen wall shrubs (*see* page 65).

Late summer to early autumn is the time take semi-ripe cuttings of climbers such as *Trachelospermum*, ivy and passion flower, as well as camellias. And take cuttings from borderline-hardy shrubs and climbers that will be left outside over winter, as an insurance against winter losses.

Also towards the end of summer, begin to collect seeds from climbers you want to propagate – pick seedheads and hang them up to dry in paper bags (*see* page 122).

Pruning

Rambling roses, which bloom on wood produced the previous season, should be pruned after flowering. Cut back old stems that have finished flowering to a younger sideshoot lower down. Well-established climbing roses that flower in a single flush on short stems should also be pruned now: remove one third of the oldest stems (*see* page 58). In late summer, prune the long, whippy shoots of wisteria, cutting them back to five or six leaves (*see* page 60).

Also prune honeysuckles that bear their flowers in whorls on old wood, cutting back each flowered shoot to a newer sideshoot. Twining climbers like clematis need tying in from time to time to keep them neat.

Deal with problems

Spray roses that are susceptible to black spot, rust and mildew. Watch out for signs of clematis wilt (*see* page 71). This can be caused by different factors, so check that the soil isn't dry and look for signs of physical damage at the base of stems that are affected. If clematis wilt is suspected, cut the affected stems back to ground level; with luck, the plant will resprout with healthy stems – but this might not be until the following spring.

Don't forget

Ensure containers do not run out of moisture. This may mean watering daily in unusually warm, dry weather. It is particularly important to water honeysuckle to prevent mildew.

Layering is a simple way to propagate clematis. Weight a stem down with a metal peg or a stone and let it take root.

Autumn

Misty autumnal mornings are a reminder that the first frosts are just around the corner and you need to think about protecting your plants. However, while the soil is still warm, it's a good time to plant new climbers and wall shrubs to fill any gaps you noticed during the summer. It is not too late to try layering some climbers or to take hardwood cuttings. You might also like to store and – in mild areas at least – sow certain seeds.

Gentle mists and cobwebs on the last of the sweet peas: sure signs that summer has given way to autumn.

Protect your plants

Take steps to protect climbers and wall shrubs. Erect windbreak netting to protect young evergreens, in particular, from cold winter winds. Borderline-hardy plants can be protected with either an insulating 'duvet' made from a double layer of netting stuffed with dry leaves or with garden fleece.

Now is a good time to insulate the roots of climbers and wall shrubs such as *Abutilon*, *Callistemon*, *Carpenteria*, evergreen ceanothus and *Trachelospermum*. The easiest method is to cover the root and crown with a 15cm (6in) deep insulating layer of dry material, such as bark chippings or straw.

Move borderline-hardy climbers and wall shrubs in containers to a sheltered part of the garden, such as by the garage or at the base of a hedge, to protect them during the winter months. Alternatively, parcel them up with an insulating layer of bubble wrap or garden fleece.

New plants

Before you buy a new plant, check it is suitable for the position you have in mind. Wait until mid-spring to plant evergreen and borderline-hardy plants. Propagate by layering suitably low and flexible stems of climbers such as *Campsis* and ivy. When grown as ground cover, ivies often root themselves, so you might find suitable ready-rooted material. Take hardwood cuttings from Russian vine (*Fallopia*), jasmine, honeysuckle and roses. In the case

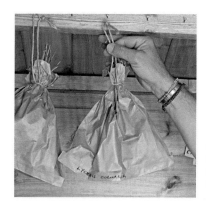

of honeysuckle, take short basal or nodal cuttings about 15cm (6in) long; with the others take cuttings 20–30cm (8–12in) long. Sow sweet peas for earlier flowering next year in mild areas only. Soak seed for 24 hours before sowing; if any remains wrinkled because it hasn't absorbed the water, nick it with a small knife. (*See also* pages 64–7.)

Don't forget

Start to collect fallen leaves from under deciduous climbers and wall shrubs. This is particularly important with disease-prone climbers, such as roses, because the diseases often overwinter on the fallen leaves, ready to infect new growth the following spring.

Check any seedheads you have hanging up. Once dry, take the seeds out of the capsules, put in envelopes and keep in a sealed container in a cool place.

Winter

Make the most of dark winter evenings by poring over books and catalogues and choosing new climbers and wall shrubs, but on days when you're tempted outside, keep active by checking the supports of climbers and wall shrubs. You might also want to take some cuttings and, yes, there's a bit of pruning you can do.

Making new plants

Take root cuttings from climbers such as *Campsis, Lathyrus, Humulus* and *Celastrus*. Cut fleshy roots into 5cm (2in) sections and insert them into pots of fresh, moist cuttings compost. There is also still time to take hardwood cuttings from climbers such as clematis and Virginia creeper (*Parthenocissus*). With clematis, take short cuttings with a pair of buds at either end, but with Virginia creeper, take cuttings around 15cm (6in) long.

Don't forget

Order seed catalogues early, if you are intending to raise annual climbers from seed next year. Make your selections and put in your order before Christmas to be sure of getting the varieties you want.

Pruning

Prune repeat-flowering climbing roses, which flower over a long period through the summer months, while they are dormant in winter. Cut back the sideshoots that have flowered to a couple of buds. Also prune wisteria, for the second time, during early winter, once the plant is fully dormant (*see* page 60). Cut the shoots pruned in summer to five or six leaves down to just two or three buds – this will improve flower production for the following year. Any new extension growth put on since the summer pruning should be cut back to about 15cm (6in). Cut back vigorous climbers such as ivies, Virginia creeper and climbing hydrangea if they have reached the limits of their support. You will need to cut them back by an additional 50cm (20in) from gutters and entrances, to allow for new growth during the coming season.

Keep on top of things

Check the supports of climbers to make sure they're in good condition and carry out any repairs that are needed. You might have to untie the climbers and carefully lower them down to the floor in order to do this. Also, make sure that

Winter is the ideal time to be putting up or repairing supports for your climbers and wall shrubs.

Garrya elliptica: to be sure you get a male plant, which produces the best winter catkins, buy when it's in flower.

all growth is firmly tied into supports, to help prevent wind damage during late-winter storms. Get ahead by putting up supports ready for the new additions. Fix trellis to walls and at the top of fences, and add horizontal wires to walls (*see* pages 50–2). Make sure you leave a sufficient gap between the support and the climber or wall shrub for adequate air circulation.

Index

Page numbers in *italics* refer to plants illustrated and/or described in the A–Z of recommended climbers and wall shrubs.

Acknowledgements

BBC Books and OutHouse would like to thank the following for their assistance in preparing this book: Candida Frith-Macdonald for help with illustrations; Andrew McIndoe and Phil McCann for advice and guidance; Joanne Forrest Smith for picture research; Lesley Riley for proofreading; June Wilkins for the index.

Picture credits

Key t = top; b = bottom; l = left; r = right; c = centre

All photographs by **Jonathan Buckley** (including the following in conjunction with National Trust Picture Library 9, 14tl, 17tr, 25t, 30b, 31tl, 50, 72) except the following:

David Austin Roses 32c, 98bl

BBC Magazines Ltd 71

Pip Bensley 78tr, 81tc & tr, 82bl, 85tc, 87bc, 93tr, 95tl

Burncoose Nurseries 40

Jonathan Edwards 79tc, 88tl, 92bc, 93bl

GAP Photos Lee Avison 96bl; BBC Magazines Ltd 30t, 119b; Dave Bevan 22(2); Richard Bloom 19(1), 36l, 88tr, 95tl, 96tl, 102tc; Christina Bollen 100br; Mark Bolton 15, 87tl, 97tl, 98tr, 112t; Elke Borkowski 13t, 16t, 53, 63(2), 80bl, 84br; Jonathan Buckley 32l, 59br; Leigh Clapp 88bl, 100tl; Sarah Cuttle 81tl; Julie Dansereau 13b; Paul Debois 83br, 101br; Carole Drake 86bl; Heather Edwards 78tl, 79br; Ron Evans 19(2), 36c, 110t; FhF Greenmedia 27(2r), 63(2), 86bc; Suzie Gibbons 10, 80tr; John Glover 37(2), 39(1 & 3), 80br, 89tr, 91tc, 92tl & tr, 94tl, 95bc, 97bc, 99, 100tc, 104tc, 111; Jerry Harpur 29(3), 76bc, 79tr, 82tl, 87tr, 98br; Marcus Harpur 18b, 80bc; Neil Holmes 22(3), 27(2l), 32r, 39(2), 76tc & bl, 89br, 98bc, 103bc, 105br, 112b, 113, 115; Michael Howes 77tc, 82tr, 110b; Martin Hughes-Jones 90tr, 102bc; Andrea Jones 38tl, 101bl; Geoff Kidd 27(1r, 3l & r), 74br; Fiona Lea 8, 78bl, 104tr; Jenny Lilly 2–3, 21r; Zara Napier 74tl; Clive Nichols 16b, 22(4), 27(4l) 93bc, 94tr; S & O 5, 20, 36r, 37(1), 73bl, 86tl, 105tc, 107, 114; Howard Rice 73tr, 90bc, 91br, 105tr & br, 108b, 116;

Rice Buckland 46t, 48; Sabina Ruber 77bc, 79bl, 83t, 85br, 87br; J S Sira 4, 27(4r), 29(1 & 2), 73c, 75bc, 80tl, 89tc, bl & bc, 101tr, 102br, 104bc, 117; Friedrich Strauss 74bl; Graham Strong 33r, 34c, 93tl; Claire Takacs 18t; Maddie Thornhill 27(1l), 28(1), 78br; Juliette Wade 23(1), 28(2), 34l & r; Mel Watson 97tc; Jo Whitworth 80tc; Rob Whitworth 35r, 102bl; Dave Zubraski 31c

John Glover 92tc, 95bc

GWIMAP/A Descat 93br

Harpur Garden Images 43t, 55t, 75br, 95bc, 102tl

Andrew McIndoe 73br, 74bc, 77tl & tr, bl & br, 79tl & bc, 81bl, bc & br, 82tc, bc & br, 83bl, 84tl & bl, 85tl, tc, tr, bl & bc, 86tc, tr & br, 87tc & bl, 88tc, bc & br, 89tl, 90tl, 92bl & br, 93br, 94tc, bc & br, 95tc, bl & br, 96tc, tr & bc, 97bl, 98tl & tc, 100tr, bl & bc, 101tl, tc & bc, 102tr, 103t, bl & br, 104tl, bl & br, 105tl, bl & bc

Pan Global Plants 74tc

Photolibrary Howard Rice 75tr, 94bl

Robin Whitecross 11(5), 43b, 46b

Roselandhouse.co.uk 91bc

Thanks are also due to the following designers and owners whose gardens appear in the book:

Margaret Archibald, Val Donnelly, Rae McNab & Coralin Pearson 78tl; Gill Brown, Valentine Cottage, Hampshire 21bl, 26; Veronica Cross, Lower Hopton Farm, Herefordshire 24bl; Paul Hervey Decorative Products 22(4); Rani Lall, Oxford, Oxfordshire 32t; Simon Mitchell, Trull House, Gloucestershire 14br; Judy Pearce, Lady Farm, Somerset 14tr; Sarah Raven, Perch Hill, East Sussex 19(3), 23(2), 66; David and Mavis Seeney, Kent 108t; The National Trust, Sissinghurst Castle Gardens, Kent 9, 14tl, 17tr, 25t, 30b, 50, 73; Carol and Malcolm Skinner, Eastgrove Cottage Garden Nursery 109; Helen Yemm, Eldenhurst, East Sussex 51t, 106

While every effort has been made to trace and acknowledge all copyright holders, the publisher would like to apologize should there be any errors or omissions.